HISTORY

OF THE

American Clock Business

FOR THE PAST SIXTY YEARS,

AND

Life of CHAUNCEY JEROME,

WRITTEN BY HIMSELF.

BARNUM'S CONNECTION

WITH THE

YANKEE CLOCK BUSINESS.

Copyright © 2013 Read Books Ltd.
This book is copyright and may not be
reproduced or copied in any way without
the express permission of the publisher in writing

British Library Cataloguing-in-Publication Data
A catalogue record for this book is available from the
British Library

A History of Clocks and Watches

Horology (from the Latin, Horologium) is the science of measuring time. Clocks, watches, clockwork, sundials, clepsydras, timers, time recorders, marine chronometers and atomic clocks are all examples of instruments used to measure time. In current usage, horology refers mainly to the study of mechanical time-keeping devices, whilst chronometry more broadly included electronic devices that have largely supplanted mechanical clocks for accuracy and precision in time-keeping. Horology itself has an incredibly long history and there are many museums and several specialised libraries devoted to the subject. Perhaps the most famous is the *Royal Greenwich Observatory*, also the source of the Prime Meridian (longitude 0° 0' 0"), and the home of the first marine timekeepers accurate enough to determine longitude.

The word 'clock' is derived from the Celtic words *clagan* and *clocca* meaning 'bell'. A silent instrument missing such a mechanism has traditionally been known as a timepiece, although today the words have become interchangeable. The clock is one of the oldest human interventions, meeting the need to consistently measure intervals of time shorter than the natural units: the day, the lunar month and the year. The current sexagesimal system of time measurement dates to approximately 2000 BC in Sumer. The Ancient Egyptians divided the day into two twelve-hour periods and used large obelisks to track the movement of the sun. They also developed water clocks, which had also been employed frequently by the Ancient Greeks, who called them 'clepsydrae'. The Shang Dynasty is also believed to have used the outflow water clock around the same time.

The first mechanical clocks, employing the verge escapement mechanism (the mechanism that controls the rate of a clock by advancing the gear train at regular intervals or 'ticks') with a foliot or balance wheel timekeeper (a weighted wheel that rotates back and forth, being returned toward its centre position by a spiral), were invented in Europe at around the start of the fourteenth century. They became the standard timekeeping device until the pendulum clock was invented in 1656. This remained the most accurate timekeeper until the 1930s, when quartz oscillators (where the mechanical **resonance** of a vibrating crystal is used to create an electrical signal with a very precise **frequency**) were invented, followed by atomic clocks after World War Two. Although initially limited to laboratories, the development of microelectronics in the 1960s made **quartz clocks** both compact and cheap to produce, and by the 1980s they became the world's dominant timekeeping technology in both clocks and **wristwatches**.

The concept of the wristwatch goes back to the production of the very earliest watches in the sixteenth century. Elizabeth I of England received a wristwatch from Robert Dudley in 1571, described as an arm watch. From the beginning, they were almost exclusively worn by women, while men used pocket-watches up until the early twentieth century. This was not just a matter of fashion or prejudice; watches of the time were notoriously prone to fouling from exposure to the elements, and could only reliably be kept safe from harm if carried securely in the pocket. Wristwatches were first worn by military men towards the end of the nineteenth century, when the importance of synchronizing manoeuvres during war without potentially revealing the plan to the enemy through signalling was increasingly recognized. It was clear that using pocket watches while in the heat of battle or while mounted on a horse was impractical, so officers began to strap the watches to their wrist.

The company H. Williamson Ltd., based in Coventry, England, was one of the first to capitalize on this opportunity. During the company's 1916 AGM it was noted that '...the public is buying the practical things of life. Nobody can truthfully contend that the watch is a luxury. It is said that one soldier in every four wears a wristlet watch, and the other three mean to get one as soon as they can.' By the end of the War, almost all enlisted men wore a wristwatch, and after they were demobilized, the fashion soon caught on - the British *Horological Journal* wrote in 1917 that '...the wristlet watch was little used by the sterner sex before the war, but now is seen on the wrist of nearly every man in uniform and of many men in civilian attire.' Within a decade, sales of wristwatches had outstripped those of pocket watches.

Now that clocks and watches had become 'common objects' there was a massively increased demand on clockmakers for maintenance and repair. Julien Le Roy, a clockmaker of Versailles, invented a face that could be opened to view the inside clockwork – a development which many subsequent artisans copied. He also invented special repeating mechanisms to improve the precision of clocks and supervised over 3,500 watches. The more complicated the device however, the more often it needed repairing. Today, since almost all clocks are now factory-made, most modern clockmakers *only* repair clocks. They are frequently employed by jewellers, antique shops or places devoted strictly to repairing clocks and watches.

The clockmakers of the present must be able to read blueprints and instructions for numerous types of clocks and time pieces that vary from antique clocks to modern time pieces in order to fix and make clocks or watches. The trade requires fine motor coordination as clockmakers must frequently work on devices with small gears and fine machinery, as well as an appreciation for the original art form. As is evident from this very short history of clocks and watches, over the centuries the items themselves have changed – almost out of recognition, but the importance of time-keeping has not. It is an area which provides a constant source of fascination and scientific discovery, still very much evolving today. We hope the reader enjoys this book.

PREFACE.

The manufacture of Clocks has become one of the most important branches of American industry. Its productions are of immense value and form an important article of export to foreign countries. It has grown from almost nothing to its present dimensions within the last thirty years, and is confined to one of the smallest States in the Union. Sixty years ago, a few men with clumsy tools supplied the demand; at the present time, with systematized labor and complicated machinery, it gives employment to thousands of men, occupying some of the largest factories of New England. Previous to the year 1838, most clock movements were made of wood; since that time they have been constructed of metal, which is not only better and more durable but even cheaper to manufacture.

Many years of my own life have been inseparably connected with and devoted to the American clock business, and the most important changes in it have taken place within my remembrance and actual experience. Its whole history is familiar to me, and I cannot write my life without having much to say about "Yankee clocks." Neither can there be a history of that business written without alluding to myself.

A few weeks since I entered my sixty-seventh year, and reviewing the past, many trying experiences are brought fresh into my mind. For more than forty-five years I have been actively engaged in the manufacture of clocks, and constantly studying and contriving new methods of manufacturing for the benefit of myself and fellow-men, and although through the instrumentality of others, I have been unfortunate in the loss of my good name and an independent competency, which I had honorably and honestly acquired by these long years of patient toil and industry, it is a satisfaction to me now to know that I have been the means of doing some good in the world.

On the following pages in my simple language, and in a bungling manner, I have told the story of my life. I am no author, but claim a title which I consider nobler, that of a "Mechanic." Being possessed of a remarkable memory, I am able to give a minute account and even the date of every important transaction of my whole life, and distinctly remember events which took place when I was but a child, three and a half years old, and how I celebrated my fourth birthday. I could relate many instances of my boyhood and later day experiences if my health and strength would permit. It has been no part of my plan to boast, exaggerate, or misrepresent anything, but to give "plain facts."

A history of the great business of Clock making has never been written. I am the oldest man living who has had much to do with it, and am best able to give its history. To-day my name is seen on millions of these useful articles in every part of the civilized globe, the result of early ambition and untiring perseverance. It was in fact the "pride of my life." Time-keepers have been known for centuries in the old world; but I will not dwell on that. It is enough for the American people to know that their country supplies the whole world with its most useful time-keepers, (as well as many other productions,) and that no other country can compete with ours in their manufacture.

It has been a long and laborious undertaking for me in my old age to write such a work as this; but the hope that it might be useful and instructive to many of my young friends has animated me to go on; and in presenting it to the public it is with the hope that it will meet with some favor, and that I shall derive some pecuniary benefit therefrom.

NEW HAVEN, August 15th, 1860.

CONTENTS.

CHAPTER I.—MY EARLY HISTORY.—Birthplace; nail making; death of my Father; leaving home; work on a farm; hard times; the great eclipse; bound out as a carpenter; carry tools thirty miles; work on clock dials; what I heard at a training; trip to New Jersey in 1812; first visit to New York; what I saw there; cross the North River in a scow; case making in New Jersey; hard fare; return home; first appearance in New Haven; at home again; a great traveller; experiences in the last war; go to New London to fight the British in 1813; incidents; soldiering at New Haven in 1814; married; hard times again; cotton cloth $1 per yard; the cold summer of 1816; a hard job; work at clocks.

CHAPTER II.—EARLY HISTORY OF YANKEE CLOCK MAKING.—Mr. Eli Terry the father of wood clocks in Connecticut; clocks in 1800; wheels made with saw and jack-knife; first clocks by machinery; clocks for pork; men in the business previous to 1810; [ ] a new invention; the Pillar Scroll Top Case; peddling clocks on horseback; the Bronze Looking Glass Clock.

CAAPTER III.—PERSONAL HISTORY CONTINUED.—1816 to 1825; work with Mr. Terry; commence business; work alone; large sale to a Southerner; a heap of money; peddle clocks in Wethersfield; walk twenty-five miles in the snow; increase business; buy mahogany in the plank; saw veneers with a hand saw; trade cases for movements; move to Bristol; bad luck; lose large sum of money; first cases by machinery in Bristol; make clocks in Mass.; good luck; death of my little daughter; form a company; invent Bronze Looking Glass Clock.

CHAPTER IV.—PROGRESS OF CLOCK MAKING.—Revival of business; Bronze Looking Glass Clock favorite; clocks at the South; $115 for a clock; rapid increase of the business; new church at Bristol—Rev. David L. Parmelee; hard times of 1837; panic in business; no more clocks will be made; wooden clocks and wooden nutmegs; opposition to Yankee pedlars in the South; make clocks in Virginia and South Carolina; my trip to the South; discouragements; "I won't give up;" invent one day Brass clock; better times ahead; go further South; return home; produce the new clock; its success.

CHAPTER V.—BRASS CLOCKS—CLOCKS IN ENGLAND.—The new clock a favorite; I carry on the business alone; good times: profits in 1841; wood clock makers half crazy; competition; prices reduced; can Yankee clocks be introduced into England; I send out a cargo; ridiculed by other clock makers; prejudice of English people against American manufacturers; how they were introduced; seized by custom house officers; a good joke; incidents; the Terry family.

CHAPTER VI.—THE CAREER OF A FAST YOUNG MAN.—Incidents; Frank Merrills; a smart young man; I sell him clocks; his bogus operations; a sad history; great losses; human nature; my experience; incident of my boyhood; Samuel J. Mills, the Missionary; anecdotes.

CHAPTER VII.—REMOVAL TO NEW HAVEN—FIRE—TROUBLE.—Make cases at New Haven; factories at Bristol destroyed by fire; great loss; sickness; heavy trouble; human nature; move whole business to New Haven; John Woodruff; great competition; clocks in New York; swindlers; law-suit; ill-feeling of other clock makers.

CHAPTER VIII.—THE METHOD OF MANUFACTURING—THE JEROME MANUFACTURING COMPANY.—Benefit of manufacturing by system; a clock case for eight cents; a clock for seventy-five cents; thirty years ago and to-day; more human nature; how the Brass clock is made; cost of a clock; the facilities of the Jerome Manufacturing Company; a joint stock company; how it was managed; interesting statements; its failure.

CHAPTER IX.—MEN NOW IN THE BUSINESS.—The New Haven Clock Co.: Hon. Jas. E. English, H. M. Welch, John Woodruff, Hiram Camp, Philip Pond, Charles L. Griswold, L. F. Root. Benedict & Burnham Company of Waterbury: Arad W. Welton. Seth Thomas & Co. Wm. L. Gilbert. E. N. Welch. Beach & Hubbell. Ireneus Atkins.

CHAPTER X.—BARNUM'S CONNECTION IN THE CLOCK BUSINESS.—Barnum and the Jerome Manufacturing Co.; Terry & Barnum; interesting statements; causes of the failure; the results.

CHAPTER XI.—EFFECTS OF THE FAILURE ON MYSELF.—My prospects; leave New Haven; move to Waterbury; a frightful accident; a practical story.

CHAPTER XII.—ANOTHER UNFORTUNATE PARTNERSHIP.—More misplaced confidence; a dishonest man threatening to imprison me for fraud; every dollar gone; kindness of John Woodruff, etc.

CHAPTER XIII.—THE WOOSTER PLACE CHURCH—Reasons for building it, and how it was built; growth of different denominations, etc.

CHAPTER XIV.—NEW HAVEN AS A BUSINESS PLACE—growth, extensive manufactories, facilities for manufacturing, population, wealth, etc.

APPENDIX.—General directions for keeping clocks in order, etc.

AMERICAN CLOCK MAKING.

LIFE OF CHAUNCEY JEROME.

CHAPTER I.

EARLY DAYS.—LEAVING HOME.—BOUND OUT.—FARMING.—CARPENTER.—SOLDIER.—CLOCK MAKING.

I was born in the town of Canaan, Litchfield County, in the State of Connecticut, on the 10th day of June, 1793. My parents were poor but respectable and industrious. My father was a blacksmith and wrought-nail maker by trade, and the father of six children—four sons and two daughters. I was the fourth child.

In January, 1797, he moved from Canaan to the town of Plymouth, in the same County, and in the following spring built a blacksmith shop, which was large enough for three or four men to work at the nail making business, besides carrying on the blacksmithing. At that time all the nails used in the country were hammered by hand out of iron rods, which practice has almost entirely been done away by the introduction of cut nails.

My advantages for education were very poor. When large enough to handle a hoe, or a bundle of rye, I was kept at work on the farm. The only opportunity I had for attending school was in the winter season, and then only about three months in the year, and at a very poor school. When I was nine years old, my father took me into the shop to work, where I soon learned to make nails, and worked with him in this way until his death, which occurred on the fifth of October, 1804. For two or three days before he died, he suffered the most excruciating pains from the disease known as the black colic. The day of his death was a sad one to me, for I knew that I should lose my happy home, and be obliged to leave it to seek work for my support. There being no manufacturing of any account in the country, the poor boys were obliged to let themselves to the farmers, and it was extremely difficult to find a place to live where they would treat a poor boy like a human being. Never shall I forget the Monday morning that I took my little bundle of clothes, and with a bursting heart bid my poor mother good bye.

I knew that the rest of the family had got to leave soon, and I perhaps never to see any of them again. Being but a boy and naturally very sympathizing, it really seemed as if my heart would break to think of leaving my dear old home for good, but stern necessity compelled me, and I was forced to obey.

The first year after leaving home I was at work on a farm, and almost every day when alone in the fields would burst into tears—not because I had to work, but because my father was dead whom I loved, and our happy family separated and broken up never to live together again. In my new place I was kept at work very hard, and at the age of fourteen did almost the work of a man. It was a very lonely place where we lived, and nothing to interest a child of my age. The people I lived with seemed to me as very old, though they were probably not more than thirty-six years of age, and felt no particular interest in me, more than to keep me constantly at work, early and late, in all kinds of weather, of which I never complained. I have many times worked all day in the woods, chopping down trees, with my shoes filled with snow; never had a pair of boots till I was more than twenty years old. Once in two weeks I was allowed to go to church, which opportunity I always improved.

I liked to attend church, for I could see so many folks, and the habit which I then acquired has never to this day left me, and my love for it dates back to this time in my youth, though the attractions now are different.

I shall never forget how frightened I was at the great eclipse which took place on the 16th of June, 1806, and which so terrified the good people in every part of the land. They were more ignorant about such operations of the sun fifty-four years ago than at the present time. I had heard something about eclipses but had not the faintest idea what it could be. I was hoeing corn that day in a by-place three miles from town, and thought it certainly was the day of judgment. I watched the sun steadily disappearing with a trembling heart, and not till it again appeared bright and shining as before, did I regain my breath and courage sufficient to whistle.

The winter before I was fifteen years old, I went to live with a house carpenter to learn the trade, and was bound to him by my guardian till I was twenty-one years old, and was to have my board and clothes for my services. I learned the business very readily, and during the last three years of my apprenticeship could do the work of a man.

It was a very pleasant family that I lived with while learning my trade. In the year 1809 my "boss" took a job in Torringford, and I went with him. After being absent several months from home, I felt very anxious to see my poor mother who lived about two miles from Plymouth. She lived alone—with the exception of my youngest brother about nine years old. I made up my mind that I would go down and see her one night. In this way I could satisfy my boss by not losing any time. It was about twenty miles, and I only sixteen years old. I was really sorry after I had started, but was not the boy to back out. It took me till nearly morning to get there tramping through the woods half of the way; every noise I heard I thought was a bear or something that would kill me, and the frightful notes of the whippoorwill made my hair stand on end. The dogs were after me at every house I passed. I have never forgotten that night. The boys of to-day do not see such times as I did.

The next year, 1810, my boss took a job in Ellsworth Society, Litchfield County. I footed it to and from that place several times in the course of the year, with a load of joiners' tools on my back. What would a boy 17 years old now think to travel thirty miles in a hot summer's day, with a heavy load of joiners' tools on his back? But that was about the only way that we could get around in those days. At that time there were not half a dozen one-horse wagons in the whole town. At that place I attended the church of Rev. Daniel Parker, father of Hon. Amasa J. Parker, of Albany, who was then a little boy four or five years old. I often saw him at meeting with his mother. He is a first cousin of F. S. & J. Parker of this city, two highly respectable men engaged in the paper business.

In the fall of 1811, I made a bargain with the man that I was bound to, that if he would give me four months in the winter of each year when the business was dull, I would clothe myself. I therefore went to Waterbury, and hired myself to Lewis Stebbins, (a singing master of that place,) to work at making the dials for the old fashioned long clock. This kind of business gave me great satisfaction, for I always had a desire to work at clocks. In 1807, when I was fourteen years old, I proposed to my guardian to get me a place with Mr. Eli Terry, of Plymouth, to work at them. Mr. Terry was at that time making more clocks than any other man in the country, about two hundred in a year, which was thought to be a great number.

My guardian, a good old man, told me that there was so many clocks then making, that the country would soon be filled with them, and the business would be good for nothing in two or three years. This opinion of that wise man made me feel very sad. I well remember, when I was about twelve years old, what I heard some old gentleman say, at a training, (all of the good folks in those days were as sure to go to training as to attend church,) they were talking about Mr. Terry; the foolish man they said, had begun to make two hundred clocks; one said, he never would live long enough to finish them; another remarked, that if he did he never would, nor could possibly sell so many, and ridiculed the very idea.

I was a little fellow, but heard and swallowed every word those wise men said, but I did not relish it at all, for I meant some day to make clocks myself, if I lived.

What would those good old men have thought when they were laughing at and ridiculing Mr. Terry, if they had known that the little urchin who was so eagerly listening to their conversation would live to make *Two Hundred Thousand* metal clocks in one year, and *many millions* in his life. They have probably been dead for years, that little boy is now an old man, and during his life has seen these great changes. The clock business has grown to be one of the largest in the country, and almost every kind of American manufactures have improved in much the same ratio, and I cannot now believe that there will ever be in the same space of future time so many improvements and inventions as those of the past half century—one of the most important in the history of the world. Everyday things with us now would have appeared to our forefathers as incredible. But returning to my story—having got myself tolerably well posted about clocks at Waterbury, I hired myself to two men to go into the state of New Jersey, to make the old fashioned seven foot standing clock-case. Messrs. Hotchkiss and Pierpont, of Plymouth, had been selling that kind of a clock without the cases, in the northern part of that State, for about twenty dollars, apiece. The purchasers, had complained to them however, that there was no one in that region that could make the case for them, which prevented many others from buying. These two men whom I went with, told them that they would get some one to go out from Connecticut, to make the case, and thought they could be made for about eighteen or twenty dollars apiece, which would then make the whole clock cost about forty dollars—not so very costly after all; for a clock was then considered the most useful of anything that could be had in a family, for what it cost. I entered into an agreement with these men at once, and a few days after, we three started on the 14th Dec., 1812, in an old lumber wagon, with provisions for the journey, to the far off Jersey. This same trip can now be made in a few hours. We were *many* days. We passed through Watertown, and other villages, and stopped the first night at Bethel. This is the very place where P. T. Barnum was born, and at about this time, of whom I shall speak more particularly hereafter. The next morning we started again on our journey, and not many hours after, arrived in Norwalk, then quite a small village, situated on Long Island Sound; at this place I saw the salt water for the first time in my life, also a small row-boat, and began to feel that I was a great traveler indeed. The following night we stopped at Stamford, which was, as I viewed it, a great place ; here I saw a few sloops on the Sound, which I thought was the greatest sight that I had ever seen. This was years before a steamboat had ever passed through the Sound. The next morning we started again for New York, and as we passed along I was more and more astonished at the wonderful things that I saw, and began to think that the world was very extensive. We did not arrive at the city until night, but there being a full moon every thing appeared as pleasant, as in the day-time. We passed down through the Bowery, which was then like a country village, then through Chatham street to Pearl street, and stopped for the night at a house kept by old Mr. Titus. I arose early the next morning and hurried into the street to see how a city looked by day-light. I stood on the corner of Chatham and Pearl for more than an hour, and I must confess that if I was ever astonished in my life, it was at that time. I could not understand why so many people, of every age, description and dress, were hurrying so in every direction. I asked a man what was going on, and what all this excitement meant, but he passed right along without noticing me, which I thought was very uncivil, and I formed a very poor opinion of those city folks. I ate nothing that morning, for I thought I could be in better business for a while at least. I wandered about gazing at the many new sights, and went out as far as the Park; at that time the workmen were finishing the interior of the City Hall. I was greatly puzzled to know how the winding stone stairs could be fixed without any seeming support and yet be perfectly safe. After viewing many sights, all of which were exceedingly interesting to me, I returned to the house where my companions were. They told me that they had just heard that the ship Macedonian, which was taken a few days before from the British by one of our ships, had just been brought into the harbor and lay off down by Burling Slip, or in that region. We went down to see her, and went on board. I was surprised and frightened to see brains and blood scattered about on the deck in every direction. This prize was taken by the gallant Decatur, but a short distance from New York. Hastening back from this sickening scene, we resumed our journey. My two companions had been telling me that we should have to cross the North River in a boat, and I did not understand how a boat could be made to carry our team and be perfectly safe, but when we arrived there, I was much surprised to see other teams that were to cross over with us, and a number of people. At that time an old scow crossed from New York City to the Jersey shore, once in about two hours. What a great change has taken place in the last forty-seven years; now large steam ferry boats are crossing and recrossing, making the trip in a few minutes. It was the first time that I had ever crossed a stream, except on a bridge, and I feared that we might upset and all be drowned, but no accident happened to us; we landed in safety, and went on our way rejoicing towards Elizabethtown. At that place I saw a regiment of soldiers from Kentucky, who were on their way to the northern frontier to fight the British. They were a rough set of fellows, and looked as though they could do a great deal of fighting. It will be remembered that this was the time of the last war with England. We passed on through Elizabethtown and Morristown to Dutch Valley, where we stopped for the night. We remained at this place a few days, looking about for a cabinet shop, or a suitable place to make the clock cases. Not succeeding, we went a mile further north, to a place called Schooler's Mountain; here we found a building that suited us. It was then the day before Christmas. The people of that region, we found, kept that day more strictly than the Sabbath, and as we were not ready to go to work, we passed Christmas day indoors feeling very lonely indeed. The next day we began operations. A young man from the lower part of New Jersey worked with me all winter. We boarded ourselves in the same building that we worked in, I doing all of the house-work and cooking, none of which was very fine or fancy, our principal food being pork, potatoes and bread, using our work-bench for a table. Hard work gave us good appetite.

We would work on an average about fifteen hours a day, the house-work not occupying much of our time. I was then only nineteen years old, and it hardly seems possible that the boys of the present day could pass through such trials and hardships, and live. We worked in this way all winter. When the job was finished, I took my little budget of clothes and started for home. I traveled the first day as far as Elizabethtown, and stopped there all night, but found no conveyance from there to New York. I was told that if I would go down to the Point, I might in the course of the day, get a passage in a sailing vessel to the city. I went down early in the morning and, after waiting till noon, found a chance to go with two men in a small sail boat. I was greatly alarmed at the strange motions of the boat which I thought would upset, and felt greatly relieved when I was again on terra firma.

I wandered about the streets of New York all that afternoon, bought a quantity of bread and cheese, and engaged a passage on the Packet Sloop Eliza, for New Haven, of her Captain Zebulon Bradley. I slept on board of her that night at the dock, the next day we set sail for New Haven, about ten o'clock in the forenoon, with a fair wind, and arrived at the long wharf in (that city) about eight o'clock the same day. I stopped at John Howe's Hotel, at the head of the wharf. This was the first time that I was ever in this beautiful city, and I little thought then that I ever should live there, working at my favorite business, with three hundred men in my employ, or that I should ever be its Mayor.—Times change.

Very early the next morning, after looking about a little, I started with my bundle of clothes in one hand, and my bread and cheese in the other, to find the Waterbury turnpike, and after dodging about for a long time, succeeded in finding it, and passed on up through Waterbury to Plymouth, walking the whole distance, and arrived home about three o'clock in the afternoon. This was my first trip abroad, and I really felt that I was a great traveler, one who had seen much of the world! What a great change has taken place in so short space of time.

Soon after I returned from my western trip, there began to be a great excitement throughout the land, about the war. It was proposed by the Governor of Connecticut, John Cotton Smith, of Sharon, to raise one or two regiments of State troops to defend it in case of invasion. One Company of one hundred men, was raised in the towns of Waterbury, Watertown, Middlebury, Plymouth and Bethlem, and John Buckingham chosen Captain, who is now living in Waterbury; the other commissioned officers of the company, were Jas. M. L. Scovill, of Waterbury, and Joseph H. Bellamy, of Bethlem. The company being composed of young men, and I being about the right age, had of course to be one of them.

Early in the Summer of 1813, the British fleet run two of our ships of war up the Thames River, near New London. Their ships being so large could not enter, but lay at its mouth. Their presence so near greatly alarmed the citizens of that city, and in fact, all of the people in the eastern part of the State. Our regiment was ordered to be ready to start for New London by the first of August. The Plymouth company was called together on Sunday, which was the first of August, and exercised on the Green in front of the church, in the fore part of the day. This unusual occurrence of a military display on the Sabbath greatly alarmed the good people of the congregation, but it really was a case of necessity, we were preparing to defend our homes from a foreign foe.

In the afternoon we attended church in a body, wearing our uniforms, to the wonder and astonishment of boys, but terrible to the old people. On Monday morning we started on a march to Hartford, sleeping that night in a barn, in the eastern part of Farmington, and reaching Hartford the next day, where we joined the other companies, and all started for New London. The first night we slept in a barn in East Hartford, and the second one in an old church in Marlboro. I remember lying on the seat of a pew, with my knapsack under my head. We arrived at New London on Saturday, marching the whole distance in the first week in August, and a hotter time I have never experienced since. We were dressed in heavy woolen clothes, carrying heavy guns and knapsacks, and wearing large leather caps. It was indeed a tedious job. We were whole days traveling what can now be done in less than as many hours, and were completely used up when we arrived there, which would not appear strange. We were immediately stationed on the high ground, back from the river, about half way between the city and the light-house, in plain view of the enemy's ships. They would frequently, when there was a favorable wind, hoist their sails and beat about in the harbor, making a splendid appearance, and practising a good deal with their heavy guns on a small American sloop, which they had taken and anchored a long distance off. The bounding of the cannon balls on the water was an interesting sight to me. The first night after our arrival, I was put on guard near the Light-house, and in plain sight of the ships. I was much afraid that the sharp shooters from their barges would take me for a target and be smart enough to hit me; and a heavy shower with thunder and lightning passing over us during the night, did not alleviate my distress. I was but a boy, only twenty years old, and would naturally be timid in such a situation, but I passed the night without being killed; it seems that was not the way that I was to die.

I soon became sick and disgusted with a soldier's life; it seemed to be too lazy and low-lived to suit me, and, as near as I could judge, the inhabitants thought us all a low set of fellows. I never have had a desire to live or be anywhere without I could be considered at least as good as the average, which failing I have now as strong as ever. We not having any battles to fight, had no opportunities of showing our bravery, and after guarding the city for forty-five days, were discharged; over which we made a great rejoicing, and returned home by the way of New Haven, which was my second visit to this city. The North and Centre Churches were then building, also, the house now standing at the North-east corner of the Green, owned then by David DeForest; stopping here over night, we pased on home to Plymouth. I had not slept on a bed since I left home, and would have as soon taken the barn floor as a good bed. This ended my first campaign.

After this I went to work at my trade, the Joiners business. I was still an apprentice; would not be twenty-one till the next June.

The War was not yet over, and in October, 1814, our Regiment was ordered by Governor Smith to New Haven, to guard the city. Col. Sanford, (father of Elihu and Harvey Sanford of this city,) commanded us. On arriving, we were stationed at the old slaughter-house, in the Eastern part of the city, at the end of Green street. All the land East of Academy street was then in farmers' lots, and planted with corn, rye and potatoes now covered with large manufactories and fine dwellings. I little thought then, that I should have the largest Clock-factory in the world, within a stone's throw of my sleeping-place, as has since proved. Nothing of much importance took place during our campaign at New Haven. The British did not land or molest us. We built a large fort on the high grounds, on the East Haven side, which commanded the

Harbor, the ruins of which can now be seen from the city. A good deal of fault was found by the officers and men with the provisions, which were very poor. When this campaign closed I was through with my military glory, and returned to my home, sick and disgusted with a soldier's life. I hope our country will not be disgraced with another war.

All of the old people will remember what a great rejoicing there was through the whole country, when peace was declared in February, 1815. I was married about that time to Salome Smith, daughter of Capt. Theophilus Smith, one of the last of the Puritanical families there was in the town; she made one of the best of wives and mothers. She died on the 6th of March, 1854. We lived together 39 years. A short time after we were married, I moved to the town of Farmington, and hired a house of Mr. Chauncey Deming to live in, and went to work for Capt. Selah Porter, for twenty dollars per month. We built a house for Maj. Timothy Cowles, which was then the best one in Farmington. I was not worth at this time fifty dollars in the world.

1815, the year after the war, was, probably the hardest one there has been for the last hundred years, for a young man to begin for himself.

Pork was sold for thirteen dollars per hundred, Flour at thirteen dollars per barrel; Molasses was sold for seventy-five cents per gallon, and brown Sugar at thirty-four cents per pound. I remember buying some cotton cloth for a common shirt, for which I paid one dollar a yard, no better than can now be bought for ten cents. I mention these things to let the young men know what a great change has taken place, and what my prospects were at that time. Not liking this place, I moved back to Plymouth. I did not have money enough to pay my rent, which however, was not due until the next May, but Mr. Deming, who by the way, was one of the richest men in the State, was determined that I should not go till I had paid him. I promised him that he should have the money when it was due, if my life was spared, and he finally consented to let me go. When it came due I walked to Farmington, fifteen miles, paid him and walked back the same day, feeling relieved and happy. I obtained the job of finishing the inside of a dwelling house, which gave me great encouragement. The times were awful hard and but little business done at anything. It would almost frighten a man to see a five-dollar bill, they were so very scarce. My work was about two miles from where I lived. My wife was confined about this time with her first babe. I would rise every morning two hours before day-light and prepare my breakfast, and taking my dinner in a little pail, bid my good wife good-by for the day, and start for my work, not returning till night. About this time the Congregational Society employed a celebrated music teacher to conduct the church singing, and I having always had a desire to sing sacred music, joined his choir and would walk a long distance to attend the singing schools at night after working hard all day. I was chosen chorister after a few weeks, which encouraged me very much in the way of singing, and was afterwards employed as a teacher to some extent, and for a long time led the singing there and at Bristol where I afterwards lived. The next summer was the cold one of 1816, which none of the old people will ever forget, and which many of the young have heard a great deal about. There was ice and snow in every month in the year. I well remember on the seventh of June, while on my way to work, about a mile from home, dressed throughout with thick woolen clothes and an overcoat on, my hands got so cold that I was obliged to lay down my tools and put on a pair of mittens which I had in my pocket. It snowed about an hour that day. On the tenth of June, my wife brought in some clothes that had been spread on the ground the night before, which were frozen stiff as in winter. On the fourth of July, I saw several men pitching quoits in the middle of the day with thick overcoats on, and the sun shining bright at the same time. A body could not feel very patriotic in such weather. I often saw men when hoeing corn, stop at the end of a row and get in the sun by a fence to warm themselves. Not half enough corn ripened that year to furnish seed for the next. I worked at my trade, and had the job of finishing the inside of a three-story house, having twenty-seven doors and a white oak matched floor to make, and did the whole for eighty-five dollars. The same work could not now be done as I did it for less than five hundred dollars. Such times as these were indeed hard for poor young men. We did not have many carpets or costly furniture and servants; but as winter approached times seemed to grow harder and harder. No work could be had. I was in debt for my little house and lot which I had bought only a short time before, near the center of Plymouth, and had a payment to make on it the next spring. I proposed going south to the city of Baltimore, to obtain work, and had already made preparations to go and leave my young family for the winter, at which I could not help feeling very sad, when I accidentally heard that Mr. Eli Terry was about to fit up his factory (which was built the year before,) for making his new Patent Shelf Clock. I thought perhaps I could get a job with him, and started immediately to see Mr. Terry, and closed a bargain with him at once. I never shall forget the great good feeling that this bargain gave me. It was a pleasant kind of business for me, and then I knew I could see my family once a week or oftener if necessary.

CHAPTER II.

PROGRESS OF CLOCK MAKING.—IMPROVEMENTS BY ELI TERRY AND OTHERS.—SHELF CLOCK.

At the beginning of this book I have said that I would give to the public a history of the AMERICAN CLOCK BUSINESS. I am now the oldest man living that has had much to do with the manufacturing of clocks, and can, I believe, give a more correct account than any other person. This great business has grown almost from nothing during my remembrance. Nearly all of the clocks used in this country are made or have been made in the small State of Connecticut, and a heavy trade in them is carried on in foreign countries. The business or manufacture of them has become so systematized of late that it has brought the prices exceedingly low, and it has long been the astonishment of the whole world how they could be made so cheap and yet be good. A gentleman called at my factory a few years ago, when I was carrying on the business, who said he lived in London, and had seen my clocks in that city, and declared that he was perfectly astonished at the price of them, and had often remarked that if he ever came to this country he would visit the factory and see for himself. After I had showed him all the different processes it required to complete a clock, he expressed himself in the strongest terms—he told me he had traveled a great deal in Europe, and had taken a great interest in all kinds of manufactures, but had never seen anything equal to this, and did not believe that there was anything made in the known world that made as much show, and at the same time was as cheap and useful as the brass clock which I was then manufacturing.

The man above all others in his day for the wood clock was Eli Terry. He was born in East Windsor, Conn., in April, 1772, and made a few old fashioned hang-up clocks in his native place before he was twenty-one years of age. He was a young man of great ingenuity and good native talent. He moved to the town of Plymouth, Litchfield county, in 1793, and commenced making a few of the same kind, working alone for several years. About the year 1800, he might have had a boy or one or two young men to help him. They would begin one or two dozen at a time, using no machinery, but cutting the wheels and teeth with a saw and jack-knife. Mr. Terry would make two or three trips a year to the New Country, as it was then called, just across the North River, taking with him three or four clocks, which he would sell for about twenty-five dollars apiece. This was for the movement only. In 1807 he bought an old mill in the southern part of the town, and fitted it up to make his clocks by machinery. About this time a number of men in Waterbury associated themselves together, and made a large contract with him, they furnishing the stock, and he making the movements. With this contract and what he made and sold to other parties, he accumulated quite a little fortune for those times. The first five hundred clocks ever made by machinery in the country were started at one time by Mr. Terry at this old mill in 1808, a larger number than had ever been begun at one time in the world. Previous to this time the wheels and teeth had been cut out by hand; first marked out with square and compasses, and then sawed with a fine saw, a very slow and tedious process. Capt. Riley Blakeslee, of this city, lived with Mr. Terry at that time, and worked on this lot of clocks, cutting the teeth. Talking with Capt. Blakeslee a few days since, he related an incident which happened when he was a boy, sixty years ago, and lived on a farm in Litchfield. One day Mr. Terry came to the house where he lived to sell a clock. The man with whom young Blakeslee lived, left him to plow in the field and went to the house to make a bargain for it, which he did, paying Mr. Terry in salt pork, a part of which he carried home in his saddle-bags where he had carried the clock. He was at that time very poor, but twenty-five years after was worth $200,000, all of which he made in the clock business.

Mr. Terry sold out his business to Seth Thomas and Silas Hoadley, two of his leading workmen, in 1810. This establishment was the leading one for several years, but other ones springing up in the vicinity, the competition became so great that the prices were reduced from ten to five dollars apiece for the bare movement. Daniel Clark, Zenas Cook and Wm. Porter, started clock-making at Waterbury, and carried it on largely for several years, but finally failed and went out of the business.

Col. Wm. Leavenworth, of the same place, was in the business in 1810, but failed, and moved to Albany, N. Y. A man by the name of Mark Leavenworth made clocks for a long time, and in the latter part of his life manufactured the Patent Shelf Clock.

Two brothers, James and Lemuel Harrison, made a few before the year 1800, using no machinery, making their wheels with a saw and knife. Sixty years ago, a man by the name of Gideon Roberts got up a few in the old way: he was an excellent mechanic and made a good article. He would finish three or four at a time and take them to New York State to sell. I have seen him many times, when I was a small boy, pass my father's house on horseback with a clock in each side of his saddle-bags, and a third lashed on behind the saddle with the dials in plain sight. They were then a great curiosity to me. Mr. Roberts had to give up this kind of business; he could not compete with machinery. John Rich of Bristol was in the business; also Levi Lewis, but gave it up in a few years. An Ives family in Bristol were quite conspicuous as clock-makers. They were good mechanics. One of them, Joseph Ives, has done a great deal towards improving the eight day brass clock, which I shall speak about hereafter.

Chauncey Boardman, of Bristol, Riley Whiting, of Winsted, and Asa Hopkins, of Northfield, were all engaged in the manufacture of the old fashioned hang-up clock. Butler Dunbar, an old schoolmate of mine, and father of Col. Edward Dunbar, of Bristol, was engaged with Dr. Titus

Merriman in the same business. They all gave up the business after a few years.

Mr. Eli Terry (in the year 1814,) invented a beautiful shelf clock made of wood, which completely revolutionized the whole business. The making of the old fashioned hang-up wood clock, about which I have been speaking, passed out of existence. This patent article Mr. Terry introduced, was called the Pillar Scroll Top Case. The pillars were about twenty-one inches long, three-quarters of an inch at the base, and three-eights at the top—resting on a square base, and the top finished by a handsome cap. It had a large dial eleven inches square, and tablet below the dial seven by eleven inches. This style of clock was liked very much and was made in large quantities, and for several years. Mr. Terry sold a right to manufacture them to Seth Thomas, for one thousand dollars, which was thought to be a great sum. At first, Terry and Thomas made each about six thousand clocks per year, but afterwards increased to ten or twelve thousand. They were sold for fifteen dollars apiece when first manufactured. I think that these two men cleared about one hundred thousand dollars apiece, up to the year 1825. Mr. Thomas had made a good deal of money on the old fashioned style, for he made a good article, and had but little competition, and controlled most of the trade.

In 1818, Joseph Ives invented a metal clock, making the plates of iron and the wheels of brass. The movement was very large, and required a case about five feet long. This style was made for two or three years, but not in large quantities.

In the year 1825, the writer invented a new case, somewhat larger than the Scroll Top, which was called the Bronze Looking-Glass Clock. This was the richest looking and best clock that had ever been made, for the price. They could be got up for one dollar less than the Scroll Top, yet sold for two dollars more.

CHAPTER III.

PERSONAL HISTORY CONTINUED.—COMMENCING BUSINESS.—SALE TO A SOUTHERNER.—REMOVAL TO BRISTOL.—FIRST SERIOUS LOSS.

I must now go back and give a history of myself, from the winter of 1816, to this time (1825.) As I said before, I went to work for Mr. Terry, making the Patent Shelf Clock in the winter of 1816. Mr. Thomas had been making them for about two years, doing nearly all of the labor on the case by hand. Mr. Terry in the mean time being a great mechanic had made many improvements in the way of making the cases. Under his directions I worked a long time at putting up machinery and benches. We had a circular saw, the first one in the town, and which was considered a great curiosity. In the course of the winter he drew another plan of the Pillar Scroll Top Case with great improvements over the one which Thomas was then making. I made the first one of the new style that was ever produced in that factory, which became so celebrated for making the patent case for more than ten years after.

When my time was out in the spring, I bought some parts of clocks, mahogany, veneers, etc., and commenced in a small shop, business for myself. I made the case, and bought the movements, dials and glass, finishing a few at a time. I found a ready sale for them. I went on in this small way for a few years, feeling greatly animated with my prosperity, occasionally making a payment on my little house. I heard one day of a man in Bristol, who did business in South Carolina, who wanted to buy a few clocks to take to that market with him. I started at once over to see him, and soon made a bargain with him to deliver twelve wood clocks at twelve dollars apiece. I returned home greatly encouraged by the large order, and went right to work on them. I had them finished and boxed ready for shipping in a short time. I had agreed to deliver them on a certain day and was to receive $144 in cash. I hired an old horse and lumber wagon of one of my neighbors, loaded the boxes and took an early start for Bristol. I was thinking all the way there of the large sum that I was to receive, and was fearful that something might happen to disappoint me. I arrived at Bristol early in the forenoon and hurried to the house of my customer, and told him I had brought the the clocks as agreed. He said nothing but went into another room with his son. I thought surely that something was wrong and that I should not get the wished-for money, but after a while the old gentleman came back and sat down by the table. "Here," he says, "is your money, and a heap of it, too." It did look to me like a large sum, and took us a long time to count it. This was more than forty years ago, and money was very scarce. I took it with a trembling hand, and securing it safely in my pocket, started immediately for home. This was a larger sum than I had ever had at one time, and I was much alarmed for fear that I should be robbed of my treasure before I got home. I thought perhaps it might be known that I was to receive a large sum for clocks, and that some robbers might be watching in a lonely part of the road and take it from me, but not meeting any, I arrived safely home, feeling greatly encouraged and happy. I told my wife that I would make another payment on our house, which I did with a great deal of satisfaction. After this I was so anxious to get along with my work that I did not so much as go out into the street for a week at a time. I would not go out of the gate from the time I returned from church one Sunday till the next. I loved to work as well as I did to eat. I remember once, when at school, of chopping a whole load of wood, for a great lazy boy, for one penny, and I used to chop all the wood I could get from the families in the neighborhood, moonlight nights, for very small sums. The winter after I made this large sale, I took about one dozen of the Pillar Scroll Top Clocks, and went to the town of Wethersfield to sell them. I hired a man to carry me over there with a lumber wagon, who returned home. I would take one of these clocks under each arm and go from house to house and offer them for sale. The people seemed to be well pleased with them, and I sold them for eighteen dollars apiece. This was good luck for me. I sold my last one on Saturday afternoon. There had been a fall of snow the night before of about eight or ten inches which ended in a rain, and made very bad walking. Here I was, twenty-five miles from home, my wife was expecting me, and I felt that I could not stay over Sunday. I was anxious to tell my family of my good luck that we might rejoice together. I started to walk the whole distance, but it proved to be the hardest physical undertaking that I ever experienced. It was bedtime when I reached Farmington, only one-third the distance, wallowing in snow porridge all the way. I did not reach home till near Sunday morning, more dead than alive. I did not go to church that day, which made many wonder what had become of me, for I was always expected to be in the singers' seat on Sunday. I did not recover from the effects of that night-journey for a long time. Soon after this occurrence, I began to increase my little business, and and employed my old joiner "boss" and one of his apprentices; bought my mahogany in the plank and sawed my own vaneers with a hand-saw. I engaged a man with a one horse wagon to go to New York after a load of mahogany, and went with him to select it. The roads were very muddy, and we were obliged to walk the whole distance home by the side of the wagon. I worked along in this small way until the year 1821, when I sold my house and lot, which I had almost worshipped, to Mr. Terry; it was worth six hundred dollars. He paid me one hundred wood clock movements, with the dials, tablets, glass and weights. I went over to Bristol to see a man by the name of George Mitchell, who owned a large two story house, with a barn and seventeen acres of good land in the southern part of the town, which he said he would sell and take his pay in clocks. I asked him how many of the Terry Patent Clocks he would sell it for; he said two hundred and fourteen. I told him I would give it, and closed the bargain at once. I finished up the hundred parts which I had got from Mr. Terry, exchanged cases with him for more, obtained some credit, and in this way made out the quantity for Mitchell.

The next summer I lost seven hundred and forty dollars by Moses Galpin of Bethlem. Five or six others with myself trusted this man Galpin with a large quantity of clocks, and he took them to Louisiana to sell in the fall of 1821. In the course of the winter he was taken sick and died there. One of his pedlars came home the next spring without one dollar in money; the creditors were called together to see what had better be done. The note that he had given me the fall before was due in July, and I as much expected it as I did the sun to rise and set. Here was trouble indeed; it was a great sum of money to lose, and what to do I didn't know. The creditors had several meetings and finally concluded to send out a man to look after the property that was scattered through the state. He could not go without money. We thought if we furnished him with means to go and finish up the business, we should certainly get enough to pay the original debt. It was agreed that we should raise a certain sum, and that each one should pay in proportion to the amount of his claim. My part was one hundred dollars, and it was a hard job for me to raise so large a sum after my great loss. When it came fall and time for him to start, I managed in some way to have it ready. This man's name was Isaac Turner, about fifty years old, and said to be very respectable. He started out and traveled all over the state, but found every thing in the worst kind of shape. The men to whom Galpin had sold would not pay when they heard that he was dead. Mr. Turner was gone from home ten months, but instead of his returning with money for us, we were obliged to pay money that he had borrowed to get home with, besides his expenses for the ten months that he was gone. This was harder for me than any of the others, and was indeed a bitter pill. As it was my first heavy loss I could not help feeling very bad.

In the winter and spring of 1822, I built a small shop in Bristol, for making the cases only, as all of the others made the movements. The first circular saw ever used there was put up by myself in 1822, and this was the commencement of making cases by machinery in that town, which has since been so renowned for its clock productions. I went on making cases in a small way for a year or two, sometimes putting in a few movements and selling them, but not making much money. The clocks of Terry and Thomas sold first rate, and it was quite difficult to buy any of the movements, as no others were making the Patent Clock at that time. I was determined to have some movements to case, and went to Chauncey Boardman, who had formerly made the old fashioned hang-up movements, and told him I wanted him to make me two hundred of his kind with such alterations as I should suggest. He said he would make them for me. I had them altered and made so as to take a case about four feet long, which I made out of pine, richly stained and varnished. This made a good clock for time and suited farmers first rate.

In the spring of 1824, I went into company with two men by the name of Peck, from Bristol. We took two hundred of these movements and a few tools in two one horse wagons and started East, intending to stop in the vicinity of Boston. We stopped at a place about fifteen miles from there called East Randolph; after looking about a little, we concluded to start our business there and hired a joiners' shop of John Adams, a cousin of J. Q. Adams. We then went to Boston and bought a load of lumber, and commenced operations. I was the case-maker of our concern, and 'pitched into' the pine lumber in good earnest. I began four cases at a time and worked like putting out fire on them. My partners were waiting for some to be finished so that they could go out and sell. In two or three days I had got them finished and they started with them, and I began four more. In a day or two they returned home having sold them at sixteen dollars *each*. This good fortune animated me very much. I worked about fourteen or fifteen hours per day, and could make about four cases and put in the glass, movements and dials. We worked on in this way until we had finished up the two hundred, and sold them at an average of sixteen dollars apiece. We had done well and returned home with joyful hearts in the latter part of June. On arriving home I found my little daughter about five years old quite sick. In a week after she died. I deeply felt the loss of my little daughter, and every 7th of July it comes fresh into my mind.

In the fall of 1824, I formed a company with my brother, Noble Jerome, and Elijah Darrow, for the manufacturing of clocks, and began making a movement that required a case about six or eight inches longer than the Terry Patent. We did very well at this for a year or two, during which time I invented the Bronze Looking Glass Clock, which soon revolutionized the whole business. As I have said before, it could be made for one dollar less and sold for two dollars more than the Patent Case; they were very showy and a little longer. With the introduction of this clock in the year 1825, closed the second chapter of the history of the Yankee Clock business.

CHAPTER IV.

THE BRONZE LOOKING GLASS CLOCK.—CHURCH AT BRISTOL.—PANIC OF 1837.—CLOCKS AT THE SOUTH.—THE ONE DAY BRASS CLOCK.

With the introduction of the Bronze Looking-Glass Clock, the business seemed to revive in all the neighboring towns, but more especially in Plymouth and Bristol. Both Mr. Terry and Mr. Thomas, did and said much in disparagement of my new invention, and tried to discourage the pedlars from buying of me, but they did as men do now-a-days, buy where they can do the best and make the most money. This new clock was liked very much in the southern market. I have heard of some of these being sold in Mississippi and Lousianna as high as one hundred and one hundred and fifteen dollars, and a great many at ninety dollars, which was a good advance on the first cost. Mr. Thomas gave out that he would not make them any how, he did not want to follow Jerome, but did finally come to it, making only a few at first, but running them down in the mean time and praising his old case. He finally gave up making the Scroll Top and made my new kind altogether.

Samuel Terry, a brother of Eli, came to Bristol about this time, and commenced making this kind of clock.

Several others began to make them—Geo. Mitchell and his brother in-law Rollin Atkins went into it, also Riley Whiting of Winsted. The business increased very rapidly between 1827 and 1837. During these ten years Jeromes and Darrow made more than any other company. The two towns of Plymouth and Bristol grew and improved very rapidly; many new houses were built, and every thing looked prosperous.

In 1831, a new church was built in Bristol, and, it is said, through the introduction of this Bronze Looking Glass Clock. Jeromes and Darrow paid one-third of the cost of its erection. The writer obtained every dollar of the subscription. The Hon. Tracy Peck and myself first started this project, which ended in building this fine church which was finished and dedicated in August, 1832. The Rev. David Lewis Parmelee preached the dedication sermon, and was the settled minister there. I was greatly interested in his preaching for ten years. He has for the last nineteen years preached at South Farms now the town of Morris. This Mr. Parmelee was a merchant till he was thirty years old, and was then converted in some mysterious manner, as St. Paul was, and left his business to preach the gospel. He proved to be one of the soundest preachers in the land, and I have no doubt but he will be one of the bright and shining lights in heaven. Oh! what happy days I saw during those ten years, little dreaming of the great troubles that were before me, or that I should experience in after life, which are now resting so heavily upon me, many times seeming greater than I can bear. But such is life.

About this time, also, Chauncey and Lawson C. Ives, two highly respectable men, built a factory in Bristol for the purpose of making an eight day brass clock. This clock was invented by Joseph Ives, a brother of Chauncey, and sold for about twenty dollars. The manufacture of these was carried on very successfully for a few years by them, but in 1836, their business was closed up, they having made about one hundred thousand dollars. Soon after this, in 1837, came the great panic and break-down of business which extended all over the country. Clock makers and almost every one else stopped business. I should mention that another company made the eight day brass clock previous to 1837, Erastus and Harvey Case and John Birge. Their clocks were retailed mostly in the southern market. They made perhaps four thousand a year. The

Ives Co., made about two thousand, but both went out of business in 1837, and it was thought that clock making was about done with in Conn.

The third chapter, as I have divided it, was now closing up. Wood clocks were good for time, but it was a slow job to properly make them, and difficult to procure wood just right for wheels and plates, and it took a whole year to season it. No factory had made over *Ten* thousand in a year; they were always classed with wooden nutmegs and wooden cucumber seeds, and could not be introduced into other countries to any advantage. But this was not the only trouble; being on water long as they would have to be, would swell the wood of the wheels and ruin the clock. Here then we had the eight day brass clock costing about twenty dollars; the idea had always been that a brass clock must be an eight day, and all one day should be of wood, and the plan of a brass one day had never been thought of.

In 1835, the southern people were greatly opposed to the Yankee pedlars coming into their states, especially the clock pedlars, and the licences were raised so high by their Legislatures that it amounted to almost a prohibition. Their laws were that any goods made in their own States could be sold without licence. Therefore clocks to be profitable must be made in those states. Chauncey and Noble Jerome started a factory in Richmond Va., making the cases and parts at Bristol, Connecticut, and packing them with the dials, glass &c. We shipped them to Richmond and took along workmen to put them together. The people were highly pleased with the idea of having clocks all made in their State. The old planters would tell the pedlars they meant to go to Richmond and see the wonderful machinery there must be to produce such articles and would no doubt have thought the tools we had there were sufficient to make a clock. We carried on this kind of business for two or three years and did very well at it, though it was unpleasant. Every one knew it was all a humbug trying to stop the pedlars from coming to their State. We removed from Richmond to Hamburg, S. C., and manufactured in the same way. This was in 1835 and '36.

There was another company doing the same kind of business at Augusta, Geo., by the name Case, Dyer, Wadsworth & Co., and Seth Thomas was making the cases and movements for them. The hard times came down on us and we really thought that clocks would no longer be made. Our firm thought we could make them if any body could, but like the others felt discouraged and disgusted with the whole business as it was then. I am sure that I had lost, from 1821 to this time, more than one hundred thousand *dollars*, and felt very much discouraged in consequence. Our company had a good deal of unsettled business in Virginia and South Carolina, and I started in the fall of 1837 for those places. Arriving at Richmond, I had a strong notion of going into the marl business. I had been down into Kent county, the summer before, where I saw great mountains of this white marl composed of shells of clams and oysters white as chalk. I had sent one vessel load of this to New Haven the year before. At Richmond I was looking after our old accounts, settling up, collecting notes and picking up some scattered clocks.

One night, I took one of these clocks into my room and placing it on the table, left a light burning near it and went to bed. While thinking over my business troubles and disappointments, I could not help feeling very much depressed. I said to myself I will not give up yet, I know more about the clock business than anything else. That minute I was looking at the wood clock on the table and it came into my mind instantly that there could be a cheap one day brass clock that would take the place of the wood clock. I at once began to figure on it;

the case would cost no more, the dials, glass, and weights and other fixtures would be the same, and the size could be reduced. I lay awake nearly all night thinking this new thing over. I knew there was a fortune in it. Many a sensible man has since told me that if I could have secured the sole right for making them for ten years, I could easily have made a million of dollars. The more I looked at this new plan, the better it appeared. My business took me to South Carolina before I could return home. I had now enough to think of day and night; this one day brass clock was constantly on my mind; I was drawing plans and contriving how they could be made best. I traveled most of the way from Richmond by stage. Arriving at Augusta, Geo., I called on the Connecticut men who were finishing wood clocks for that market, and told Mr. Dyer the head man, that I had got up, or could get up something when I got home that would run out all the wood clocks in the country, Thomas's and all; he laughed at me quite heartily. I told him that was all right, and asked him to come to Bristol when he went home and I would show him something that would astonish him. He promised that he would, and during the next summer when he called at my place, I showed him a shelf full of them running, which he acknowledged to be the best he had ever seen.

I arrived home from the south the 28th of January, and told my brother who was a first-rate clock maker what I had been thinking about since I had been gone. He was much pleased with my plan, thought it a first rate idea, and said he would go right to work and get up the movement, which he perfected in a short time so that it was the best clock that had ever been made in this or any other country. There have been more of this same kind manufactured than of any other in the United States. What I originated that night on my bed in Richmond, has given work to thousands of men yearly for more than twenty years, built up the largest manufactories in New England, and put more than a million of dollars into the pockets of the brass makers,—" but there is not one of them that remembers *Joseph.*"

CHAPTER V.

SUCCESS OF THE NEW INVENTION.—INTRODUCTION OF CLOCKS IN ENGLAND.—TERRY FAMILY, ETC.

We went on very prosperously making the new clock, and it was admired by every body. In the year 1839, some of my neighbors and a few of my leading workmen had a great desire to get into the same kind of business. We knew competition amongst Yankees was almost sure to kill business and proposed to have them come in with us and have a share of the profits. An arrangement to this effect was made and we went on in this way until the fall of 1840. I found they were much annoyance and bother to me, and so bought them all out, but had to give them one hundred per cent. for the use of their money. Some of them had not paid in anything, but I had to pay them the same profits I did the rest, to get rid of them. One man had put in three thousand dollars for which I paid him six thousand. I also bought out my brother Noble Jerome, who had been in company with me for a long time, and carried on the whole business alone, which seemed to be rapidly improving.

I made in 1841, thirty-five thousand dollars clear profits. Men would come and deposit money with me before their orders were finished. This successful state of things set all of the wood clock makers half crazy, and they went into it one after another as fast as they could, and of course run down the price very fast—"Yankee-like." I had been thinking for two or three years of introducing my clocks into England, and had availed myself of every opportunity to get posted on that subject; when I met Englishmen in New York and other places, I would try to find out by them what the prospects would be for selling Yankee clocks in their country. I ascertained that there were no cheap metal clocks used or known there, the only cheap timepiece they had was a Dutch hang-up wood clock.

In 1842, I determined to make the venture of sending a consignment of brass clocks to Old England. I made a bargain with Epaphroditus Peck, a very talented young man of Bristol, a son of Hon. Tracy Peck, to take them out, and sent my son Chauncey Jerome, Jr. with him. All of the first cargo consisted of the O. G. one day brass clocks. As soon as it was known by the neighboring clock-makers, they laughed at me, and ridiculed the idea of sending clocks to England where labor was so cheap. They said that they never would interfere with Jerome in that visionary project, but no sooner had I got them well introduced, after spending thousands of dollars to effect it, than they had all forgotten what they said about my folly, and one after another sent over the same goods to compete with me and run down the price. As I have said before, wood clocks could never have been exported to Europe from this country, for many reasons. They would have been laughed at, and looked upon with suspicion as coming from the wooden nutmeg country, and classed as the same. They could not endure a long voyage across the water without swelling the parts and rendering them useless as time-keepers; experience had taught us this, as many wood clocks on a passage to the southern market, had been rendered unfit for use for this very reason. Metal clocks can be sent any where without injury. Millions have been sent to Europe, Asia, South America, Australia, Palestine, and in fact, to every part of the world; and millions of dollars brought into this country by this means, and I think it not unfair to claim the honor of inventing and introducing this low-price time-piece which has given employment to so many of our countrymen, and has also, been so useful to the world at large. No family is so poor but that they can have a time-piece which is both useful and ornamental. They can be found in every civilized portion of the globe. Meeting a sea captain one day, he told me that on landing at the lonely island of St. Helena, the first thing that he noticed on entering a house, was my name on the face of a brass clock. Many years ago a missionary (Mr. Ruggles,) at the Sandwich Islands, told me that he had one of my clocks in his house, the first one that had ever been on the islands. Travelers have mentioned seeing them in the city of Jerusalem, in many parts of Egypt, and in fact, every where, which accounts could not but be interesting and gratifying to me.

It was a long and tedious undertaking to introduce my first cargo in England. Mr. Peck and my son wrote me a great many times the first year, that they never could be sold there, the prejudice against American manufactures was so great that they would not buy them. Although very much discouraged, I kept writing them to 'stick to it.' They were once turned out of a store in London and threatened if they offered their "Yankee clocks" again to the English people "who made clocks for the world;" "they were good for nothing or they could not be offered so cheap." They were finally introduced in this way; the young men persuaded a merchant to take two into his store for sale. He reluctantly gave his consent, saying he did not believe they would run at all; they set the two running and left the price of them. On calling the next day to see how they were getting along, and what the London merchant thought of them, they were surprised to find them both gone. On asking what had become of them, they were told that two men came in and liked their looks and bought them. The merchant said he did not think any one would ever buy them, but told them they might bring in four more; "I will see" he says, "if I can sell any *more* of your Yankee clocks." They carried them in and calling the next day, found them all gone. The merchant then told them to bring in a dozen. These went off in a short time, and not long after, this same merchant bought two hundred at once, and other merchants began to think they could make some money on these Yankee clocks and the business began to improve very rapidly. There are always men enough who are ready to enter into a business after it is started and looks favorable. A pleasing incident occurred soon after we first started. The Revenue laws of England are (or were, at that time) that the owner of property passing through the Custom-house shall put such a price on his goods as he pleases, knowing that the government officers have a right to take the property by adding ten per cent. to the invoiced price.

I had always told my young men over there to put a fair price on the clocks, which they did; but the officers thought they put them altogether too low, so they made up their minds that they would take a lot, and seized one ship-load, thinking we would put the prices of the next cargo at higher rates. They paid the cash for this cargo, which made a good sale for us. A few days after, another invoice arrived which our folks entered at the same prices as before; but they were again taken by the officers paying us cash and ten per cent. in addition, which was very satisfactory to us. On the arrival of the third lot, they began to think they had better let the Yankees sell their own goods and passed them through unmolested, and came to the conclusion that we could make clocks much better and cheaper than their own people. Their performance has been considered a first-rate joke to say the least. There will, in all probability, be millions of clocks sold in that country, and we are the people who will furnish all Europe with all their common cheap ones as long as time lasts.

All of the spring and eight day clocks have grown out of the one day weight clock. There can now be as good an eight day clock bought for three or four dollars, as could be had for eighteen or twenty dollars before I got up the one day clock. Mr. Peck, who went to England with my son, died in London on the 20th, September, 1857; my son died in this country in July, 1853: so they have gone the way of all the earth, and I shall have to follow them soon. They were instrumental in laying the foundation of a large and prosperous business which is now being successfully carried on. The duties on clocks to England have been recently removed, which will result to the advantage of persons now in the business. The many difficulties which we had to battle and contend with are all overcome. When I invented this one day brass clock, I for the first time put on the zinc dial which is now universally used, and is a great improvement on the wood dial, both in appearance and in cost. This simple idea has been of immense value to all clock-makers.

In the year 1821, when I moved to Bristol, no one was making clocks in that town; the business had all passed away from there and was carried on in Plymouth. The little shop I had put up had no machinery in it at that time. I soon began to make so many cases that I wanted some better way to get my veneers than to saw them by hand. I found a small building on a stream some distance from my shop which I secured, with the privilege of putting a circular saw in the upper part, but which I could not use till night—the power being wanted for the other machinery during the day. I have worked there a great many nights till twelve o'clock and even two in the morning, sawing veneers for my men to use the next day. I sawed my hand nearly off one night when alone at this old mill, and was so faint by the loss of blood that I could hardly reach home. I always worked hard myself and managed in the most economical manner possible. In 1825, we built a small factory on the stream below the shop where I sawed my veneers two or three years before, but there was no road to it or bridge across the stream. I had crossed it for years on a pole, running the risk many times when the water was high, of being drowned, but it seems I was not to die in that way, but to live to help others and make a slave of myself for them. In 1826, we petitioned the town to lay out a road by our factory and build a bridge, which was seriously objected to. We finally told them that if they would lay out the road, we would build the bridge and pay for one half of the land for the road, which, after a great deal of trouble, was agreed to, and proved to be of great benefit to the town. Our business was growing very rapidly and a number of houses were built up along the new road and about our factory. I should here mention that Mr. Eli Terry, Jr., when I had got the Bronze Looking-Glass Clock well a going, moved from Plymouth Hollow two miles east of Plymouth Centre, (now the village of Terryville,) where he built another factory and went into business. His father retiring about this time, he took all of his old customers. He was a good business man and made money very fast. He was taken sick and died when about forty years old, leaving an estate of about $75,000. His brother, Silas B. Terry, is now living, a christian gentleman, as well as a scientific clock-maker, but he has not succeeded so well as his brother in making money. Henry Terry of Plymouth, who is another son of Mr. Eli Terry, was engaged in the clock business thirty years ago, but left it for the woolen business. I think that he is sorry that he did not continue making clocks. He is a man of great intelligence and understands the principles of a right tariff as well as any man in Connecticut. His father was a great man, a natural philosopher, and almost an Eli

Whitney in mechanical ingenuity. If he had turned his mind towards a military profession, he would have made another General Scott, or towards politics, another Jefferson; or, if he had not happened to have gone to the town of Plymouth, I do not believe there would ever have been a clock made there. He was the great originator of wood clock-making by machinery in Connecticut. I like to see every man have his due. Thomas and many others who have made their fortunes out of his ingenuity, were very willing to talk against him, for they must, of course, act out human nature. Seth Thomas was in many respects a first-rate man. He never made any improvements in manufacturing; his great success was in money making. He always minded his own business, was very industrious, persevering, honest, his word was as good as his note, and he always determined to make a good article and please his customers. He had several sons who are said to be smart business men.

I knew Mrs. Thomas well when I was a boy, fourteen years old. She is one of the best of women, and is now the widow of one of the richest men in the state. The families of Terry and Thomas are extensively known, throughout the United States. Mr. Thomas died two years ago at the age of seventy-five. He was born in West Haven, about four miles from New Haven, and learned the joiners' trade in Wolcott, and worked in that region and in Plymouth five or six years, building houses and barns. I waited on him when he built a barn in Plymouth, carrying boards and shingles. He soon after went into the clock business in which he remained during life. Mr. Terry died in 1853, at the advanced age of eighty-one.

CHAPTER VI.

OPERATIONS OF FRANK MERRILLS—A SAD HISTORY.—BUSINESS TROUBLES, ETC.

In the fall, of the year 1840, a young man by the name of Franklin Merrills was introduced to me as one the smartest and likeliest business men in the whole country. It was said that he could trade in horses, cattle, sheep, wool, flour, or any thing else, and make money. He belonged to one of the first families in Litchfield county. I thought by his appearance and recommendations that he would be a good customer for me and I sold him a thousand dollars worth of clocks to begin with. He gave me his four months' note which was promptly paid when due. He hired three pedlars and went with them into Dutchess county New York, where, they sold the clocks very fast. The one-day O. G. brass clock was a new thing to them, first-rate for time, and they readily went off for fifteen and twenty dollars apiece. I sold them to him for six dollars apiece, and it appeared, at this rate, that he could make a fortune in a few years. His credit became established for any amount, and he soon began to want clocks about twice as fast as at first. A man by the name of Bates transported them for him in a large two-horse wagon from my place to Washington Hollow, about twelve miles east of Poughkeepsie. Mr. Bates lived in the same neighborhood where Frank was brought up in New Hartford, Conn. Every week or two he would go out with a load. Things moved on in this seemingly prosperous way for some time. One day I accidentally heard that parties in New York with whom I had never dealt, were selling my clocks at very reduced prices, and I began to mistrust that Frank had been selling to them at less than cost. On seeing him, he told me I was greatly mistaken and smoothed down the matter so that it appeared satisfactory to me. He had at this time got into debt about eighteen thousand dollars. One day he went to Hartford and bought seven thousand dollars worth of cotton cloth from a shrewd house in that city, telling them a very fine story that he had a vessel which would sail for South America the next day, and that the cloth must go down immediately on the boat. He told them who his father was, and promised to bring his endorsement in a few days, which was satisfactory to them, and they let him have the goods. But the paper did not come. One of the firm went to New York and there found some of the goods in an Auction store, and a part of them sold. He got out a writ and arrested Frank. His father was sent for, and settled this matter satisfactorily. I thought I would go up to New Hartford and see Capt. Merrills about Frank's affairs—he told me all about them, and said he had been looking over Frank's business very thoroughly, and found that a large amount was owing him and that Frank had shown him on his book invoices of a large amount of goods that he had shipped to South America, besides several large accounts and notes—one of eight thousand dollars. He told me that he thought after paying me and others whom he owed, there would be as much as twenty thousand dollars left. This was very satisfactory to me, though I knew nothing about the cotton cloth speculation at that time. If I had, it would have saved me a great deal of trouble. This was in February, 1844. There was a note of his lying over, unpaid, in the Exchange Bank in Hartford, of two thousand dollars. I had moved a few weeks before this to New Haven. In the latter part of February, I went down to New York to see if he could let me have the two thousand to take up the note;

he said he could in a day or two. I told him I would stay till Saturday. On that day he was not able to pay me, but would certainly get it Monday, and urged me to stay over, which I did. He took me into a large establishment with him, and, as I have since had reason to believe, talked with parties who were interested with him, about consigning to them a large quantity of tallow, beeswax and wool which he owned in the West. He told me that he had some trouble with his business, and that all he wanted was a little help; he said he had a great deal of property in New York State, and that if he could raise some money, he could make a very profitable speculation on a lot of wool which he knew about. He told me that if I would give him my notes and acceptances to a certain amount, he would secure me with the obligations of Henry Martin, one of the best farmers there was in Dutchess county. He also gave the names of several merchants in New York who were acquainted with the rich farmers. I called on them and all spoke very highly of him. I thought, there could be no great risk in doing it, for my confidence in Frank was very great. I thought, of course, this would insure my claim of eighteen thousand dollars, but it eventually proved to be a deep-laid plot to swindle me. Frank had no notes or accounts that were of any value; they were all bogus and got up to deceive his poor old father and others. He had no property shipped to South America. It was all found out, when too late, that he had ruined himself by gambling and bad company, often losing a thousand dollars in one night. He was arrested, taken before the Grand Jury of New York, committed to jail for swindling, and died in a few months after. He ruined his father, who was a very cautious man, ruined three rich farmers of Dutchess county, and came very near ruining me. It was a sad history and mortifying to a great many. I was advised by my counsel, Seth P. Staples of New York, to contest the whole thing in law. I had five or six suits on my hands at one time, and it was nine years before I was clear from them. What he owed me for clocks, and what I had to pay on notes and acceptances and the expenses of law, amounted to more than *Forty Thousand Dollars*. Nine years of wakeful nights of trouble, grief and mortification, for this profligate young man! There never was a man more honest than I was in my intentions to help him in his troubles, and I am quite sure no man got so badly swindled. Every clock maker in the state would have been glad to have sold to him as I did. This young man was well brought up, but bad company ruined him and others with him. This life seems to be full of trials. In latter years I have remembered what an old man often told me when a boy. "Chauncey," he says, "don't you know there are a thousand troubles and difficulties?" I told him I did not know there were; "well," he says, "you will find out if you live long enough." I have lived long enough to see ten thousand troubles, and have found out that the saying of the old man is true. I have narrated but a small part of my business troubless in this brief history. One of the most trying things to me now, is to see how I am looked upon by the community since I lost my property. I never was any better when I owned it than I am now, and never behaved any better. But how different is the feeling towards you, when your neighbors can make nothing more out of you, politically or pecuniarily. It makes no difference what, or how much you have done for them heretofore, you are passed by without notice now. It is all money and business, business and money which make the man now-a-days; success is every thing, and it makes very little difference how, or what means he uses to obtain it. How many we see every day that have ten times as much property as they will ever want, who will do any thing but steal to add to their estate, for somebody to fight about when they are dead. I see men every day sixty and seventy years old, building up and pulling down, and preparing, as one might reasonably suppose, to live here forever. Where will they be in a few years? I often think of this. My experience has been great,—I have seen many a man go up and then go down, and many persons who, but a few years ago, were surrounded with honors and wealth, have passed away. The saying of the wise man is true—all is "vanity of vanities" here below. It is now a time of great action in the world but not much reflection.

An incident of my boy-hood has just come into my mind. When an apprentice boy, I was at work with my "boss" on a house in Torringford, very near the residence of Rev. Mr. Mills, the father of Samuel J. Mills the missionary. This was in 1809, fifty-one years ago. This young man was preparing to go out on his missionary voyage. How wickedly we are taught when we are young! I thought he was a mean, lazy fellow. He was riding out every day, as I now suppose, to add to his strength. An old maid lived in the house where I did who perfectly hated him, calling him a good-for-nothing fellow. I, of course, supposed that she knew all about him and that it was so. I am a friend to the missionary cause and have been so a great many years. How many times that wrong impression which I got from that old maid has passed through my mind, and how sorry I have always been for that prejudice. The father of Samuel J. Mills was a very eccentric man and anecdotes of him have been repeatedly told. I attended his church the summer I was in Torringford. He was the strangest man I ever saw, and would say so many laughable things in his sermon that it was next to impossible for me to keep from laughing out loud. His congregation was composed mostly of farmers, and in hot weather they appeared to be very sleepy. The boys would sometimes play and make a good deal of noise, and one Sunday he stopped in the middle of his sermon and looking around in the gallery, said in a loud voice, "boys, if you don't stop your noise and play, you will certainly wake your parents that are asleep below!" I think by this time the good people were all awake; it amused me very much and I have often seen the story printed. Many a time when I think of Mr. Mills, an anecdote of him comes into my mind, and I presume that a great many have heard of the same. He was once traveling through the town of Litchfield where there was at that time a famous law school. Two or three of the students were walking a little way out of town, when who should they see coming along the road but old Mr. Mills. They supposing him to be some old "codger," thought they would have a little fun with him. When they met him one of them asked him "if he had heard the news?" "No," he says, "what is it?" "The devil is dead." "Is he?" says Mr. Mills, "I am sorry for you— poor fatherless children, what will become of you?" I understand that they let him pass without further conversation. He was a good man and looked very old to me, as he always wore a large white wig.

CHAPTER VII.

REMOVAL TO NEW HAVEN. — FACTORY AT BRISTOL DESTROYED BY FIRE. — OTHER TROUBLES, ETC.

In the winter of 1844, I moved to the city of New Haven with the expectation of making my cases there. I had fitted up two large factories in Bristol for making brass movements only the year before, and had spared no pains to have them just right. My factory in New Haven was fitted up expressly for making the cases and boxing the finished clocks; the movements were packed, one hundred in a box, and sent to New Haven where they were cased and shipped. Business moved on very prosperously for about one year. On the 23d of April 1845, about the middle of the afternoon one of my factories in Bristol took fire, as it was supposed by some boys playing with matches at the back side of the building, which set fire to some shavings under the floor. It seemed impossible to put it out and it proved to be the most disastrous fire that ever occurred in a country town. There were seven or eight buildings destroyed, together with all the machinery for making clocks, which was very costly and extensive. There were somewhere between fifty and seventy-five thousand brass movements in the works, a large number of them finished, and worth one dollar apiece. The loss was about fifty thousand dollars and the insurance only ten thousand. This was another dark day for me. I had been very sick all winter with the Typhus fever, and from Christmas to April had not been able to go to Bristol. On the same night of the fire, a man came to tell me of the great loss. I was in another part of the house when he arrived with the message, but my wife did not think it prudent to inform me then, but in the latter part of the night she introduced a conversation that was calculated to prepare my mind for the sad news, and in a cautious manner informed me. I was at that time in the midst of my troubles with Frank Merrills, had been sick for a long time, and at one time was not expected to recover. I was not then able to attend to business and felt much depressed on that account. It was hard indeed to grapple with so much in one year, but I tried to make the best of it and to feel that these trials, troubles and disappointments sent upon us in this world, are blessings in disguise. Oh! if we could really feel this to be so in all of our troubles, it would be well for us in this world and better in the next. I never have seen the real total depravity of the human heart show itself more plainly or clearly than it did when my factories were destroyed by fire. An envious feeling had always been exhibited by others in the same business towards me, and those who had made the most out of my improvements and had injured my reputation by making an inferior article, were the very ones who rejoiced the most then. Not a single man of them ever did or could look me in the face and say that I had ever injured him. This feeling towards me was all because I was in their way and my clocks at that time were preferred before any others. They really thought I never could start again, and many said that Jerome would never make any more clocks. I learned this maxim long ago, that when a man injures another unreasonably, to act out human nature he has got to keep on misrepresenting and abusing him to make himself appear right in the sight of the world. Soon after the fire in Bristol I had gained my strength sufficiently to go ahead again, and commenced to make additions to my case factory in New Haven (to make the movements,) and by the last of June was ready to commence operations on the brass movements. I then brought my men from Bristol—the movement makers—and a noble set of men as ever came into New Haven at one time. Look at John Woodruff; he was a young man then of nineteen. When he first came to work for me at the age of fifteen, I believed that he was destined to be a leading man. He is now in Congress (elected for the second time,) honest, kind, gentlemanly, and respected in Congress and out of Congress. Look at him, young men, and pattern after him, you can see in his case what honesty, industry and perseverance will accomplish.

There was great competition in the business for several years after I moved to New Haven, and a great many poor clocks made. The business of selling greatly increased in New York, and within three or four years after I introduced the one day brass clock, several companies in Bristol and Plymouth commenced making them. Most of them manufactured an inferior article of movement, but found sale for great numbers of them to parties that were casing clocks in New York. This way of managing proved to be a great damage to the Connecticut clock makers. The New York men would buy the very poorest movements and put them into cheap O. G. cases and undersell us. Merchants from the country, about this time, began to buy clocks with their other goods. They had heard about Jerome's clocks which had been retailed about the country, and that they were good time-keepers, and would enquire for my clocks. These New York men would say that they were agents for Jerome and that they would have a plenty in a few days, and make a sale to these merchants of Jerome clocks. They would then go to the Printers and have a lot of labels struck off and put into their cheap clocks, and palm them off as mine. This fraud was carried on for several years. I finally sued some of these blackleg parties, Samuels & Dunn, and Sperry & Shaw, and found out to my satisfaction that they had used more than two hundred thousand of my labels. They had probably sent about one hundred thousand to Europe. I sued Samuels & Dunn for twenty thousand dollars and when it came to trial I proved it on them clearly. I should have got for damages fifteen thousand dollars, had it not been for one of the jury. One was for giving me twenty thousand, another Eighteen, and the others down to seven thousand five hundred. This one man whom I speak of, was opposed to giving me anything, but to settle it, went as high as two thousand three hundred. The jury thought that I had a great deal of trouble with this case and rather than have it go to another court, had to come to this man's terms. The foreman told me afterwards that he had no doubt but this man was bought. New York is a hard place to have a law suit in. This cheat had been carried on for years, both in this country and in Europe,—using my labels and selling poor articles, and in this way robbing me of my reputation by the basest means. After this Sperry, who was in company with Shaw, had been dead a short time, a statement was published in the New York papers that this Henry Sperry was a wonderful man, and that he was the first man who went to England with Yankee clocks. After I had sent over my two men and had got my clocks well introduced, and had them there more than a year, Sperry & Shaw, hearing that we were doing well and selling a good many, thought they would take a trip to Europe, and took along perhaps fifty boxes of clocks. I have since heard that their conduct was very bad while there, and this is all they did towards introducing clocks. There is no one who can claim any credit of introducing American clocks into that country excepting myself. After I had opened a store in New York, we did, in a measure, stop these men from using my labels.

I have said that when I got up this one day

brass clock in 1838, that the fourth chapter in the Yankee clock business had commenced. Perhaps Seth Thomas hated as bad as any one did to change his whole business of clock making for the second time, and adopt the same thing that I had introduced. He never invented any thing new, and would now probably have been making the same old hang-up wood clocks of fifty years ago, had it not been for others and their improvements. He was highly incensed at me because I was the means of his having to change. He hired a man to go around to my customers and offer his clocks at fifty and seventy-five cents less than I was selling. A man by the name of J. C. Brown carried on the business in Bristol a long time, and made a good many fine clocks, but finally gave up the business. Elisha Monross, Smith & Goodrich, Brewster & Ingraham were all in the same business, but have given it up, and the clock making of Connecticut is now mostly done in five large factories in different parts of the State, about which I shall speak hereafter.

CHAPTER VIII.

FURTHER IMPROVEMENTS IN CHEAP TIME-KEEPERS.
—THE PROCESS OF CLOCK MAKING.—

It would be no doubt interesting to a great many to know what improvements have been made in manufacturing clocks during the past twenty years. I recollect I paid for work on the O. G. case one dollar and seventy-five cents; for the same work in 1855, I paid twenty cents, and many other things in the same proportion. The last thing that I invented, which has proved to be of great usefulness, was the one day time-piece that can be sold for seventy-five cents, and a fair profit at that. I remember well when I was about to give up the job, of asking the man who made the cases for the factory what he would make this case for. He said he could not do it for less than eight cents, I told him I knew he could make them for five cents, and do well, but he honestly thought he could not. He was to make two thousand per month—twenty-four thousand a year. After getting the work well systematized, I told him if he could not make them at that price, I would make it up to him at the end of the year. When the time was up, he told me that it was the best part of his job, and that he would make them the next year for four cents; it will be well understood that this was for the work alone, the stock being furnished.

When I got up this new time-keeper, as usual all the clock-makers were down on me again; Jerome was going to ruin the business, and this cheap thing would take the place of larger ones. I told them there were ten thousand places where this cheap time-piece would be useful, and where a costly striking one would never be used. There is a variety of places where they are as useful as if they struck the hour, and there are now more of the striking clocks wanted than there were when I got up this one day time-piece. When I first began to make clocks, thousands would say that they could not afford to have a clock in their house and they must get along without, or with a watch. This cheap time-piece is worth as much as a watch that would cost a hundred dollars, for all practical purposes, as far as the time of day or night is concerned. Since I began to make clocks, the price has gradually been going down. Suppose the cheap time-keeper had been invented thirty years ago, when folks felt as though they could not have a clock because it cost so much, but must get along with a watch which cost ten or fifteen dollars, what would the good people have thought if they could have had a clock for one dollar, or even less? This cheap clock is much better adapted to the many log cabins and cheap dwellings in our country than a watch of any kind, and it is not half so costly or difficult to keep in order. I can think of nothing ever invented that has been so useful to so many. We do not fully appreciate the value of such things. I have often thought, that if all the time-pieces were taken out of the country at once, and every factory stopped making them, the whole community would be brought to see the incalculable value that this Yankee clock making is to them.

The little octagon marine case which is seen almost every where, was originated and first made by me. I think it is the cheapest and best looking thing of the kind in the market, and all the work on the case of that clock costs but eight cents. All of the large hang-up octagons and time-pieces were made at our factory two or three years before any other parties made them at all. As usual, after finding that it was a good thing and took well, many others began to make them. I will say here a little more about human nature and what I have seen and experienced, during the last forty-five years. Let an ingenious, thinking man invent something that looks favorable for making money, and one after another will be stealing into the same business, when they know their conduct is very mean towards the originator who may be one of the best men in the community; still, nine out of ten of those who are infringing on his improvement will begin to hate and abuse him. I have seen this disposition carried out all my life-time. Forty-five years ago, Mr. Eli Terry was the great man in the wood clock business. As I have said before, he got up the Patent Wood Shelf Clock and sold a right to make it to Seth Thomas for one thousand dollars. After two or three years, Mr. Terry made further improvements and got them patented. Mr. Thomas then thought as he had paid a thousand dollars, he would use these improvements; so he went on making the new patent. Mr. Terry sued him and the case was in litigation for several years. The whole Thomas family, the workmen and neighbors, felt envious towards Mr. Terry, and I think they have never got entirely over it. There was a general prejudice and hatred towards Mr. Terry amongst all the clock-makers at that time, and for nothing only because they knew they were infringing on his rights; and to act out human nature, they must slander and try to put him down. This principle is carried out very extensively in this world, so that if a man wants to live and have nothing said against him, he must look out for, and help no one but himself. If he succeeds in making money, it matters but little in what way he obtains it, whether by gambling or any other unlawful means; while on the other hand, if he has been doing good all his life, and by some mishap is reduced to poverty in his old age, he is despised and treated with contempt by a majority of the community.

It may not be uninteresting to a great many to know how the brass clocks at the present day are made. It has been a wonder to the world for a long time, how they could possibly be sold so cheap and yet answer so good a purpose. And, indeed, they could not, if every part of their manufacture was not systematized in the most perfect manner and conducted on a large scale. I will describe the manner in which the O-G. case is made, (the style has been made a long time, and in larger numbers than any other,) which will give some idea with what facility the whole thing is put through. Common merchantable pine lumber is used for the body of the case. The first workman draws a board of the stuff on a frame and by a movable circular saw cuts it in proper lengths for the sides and top. The knotty portions of it are sawed in lengths suitable for boxing the clocks when finished, and but little need be wasted. The good pieces are then taken to another saw and split up in proper widths, which are then passed through the planeing machine. Then another workman puts them through the O-G. cutter which forms the shape of the front of the case. The next process is the glueing on of the veneers—the workman spreads the glue on one piece at a time and then puts on the veneer of rosewood or mahogany. A dozen of these pieces are placed together in hand-screws till the glue is properly hardened. The O-G. shapes of these pieces fit into each other when they are screwed together. When the glue is sufficiently dry, the next thing is to make the veneer smooth and fit for varnishing. We have what is called a sand paper wheel, made of pine plank, its edge formed in an O-G. shape, and sand-paper glued to it. When this wheel is revolving rapidly, the pieces are passed over it and in this way smoothed very fast. They are then ready to varnish, and it usually takes about ten days to put on the several coats of varnish, and polish them ready for mitering, which completes the pieces ready for glueing in shape of the case. The sides of the case are made much cheaper. I used to have the stuff for ten thousand of these cases in the works at one time. With these great facilities, the labor costs less than twenty cents apiece for this kind of case, and with the stock, they cost less than fifty cents. A cabinet maker could not make one for less than five dollars. This proves and shows what can be done by system. The dials are cut out of large sheets of zinc, the holes punched by machinery, and then put into the paint room, where they are painted by a short and easy process. The letters and figures are then printed on. I had a private room for this purpose, and a man who could print twelve or fifteen hundred in a day. The whole dial cost me less than five cents. The tablets were printed in the same manner, the colors put on afterwards by girls, and the whole work on these beautiful tablets cost less than one and a half cents: the cost of glass and work was about four cents. Every body knows that all of these parts must be made very cheap or an O-G. clock could not be sold for one dollar and a half, or two dollars. The weights cost about thirteen cents per clock, the cost of boxing them about ten cents, and the first cost of the movements of a one-day brass clock is less than fifty cents. I will here say a little about the process of making the wheels. It will no doubt, astonish a great many to know how rapidly they can be made. I will venture to say, that I can pick out three men who will take the brass in the sheet, press out and level under the drop, there cut the teeth, and make all of the wheels to five hundred clocks in one day; there are from eight to ten of these wheels in every clock, and in an eight-day clock more. This will look to some like a great story, but is one of the wonders of the clock business. If some of the parts of a clock were not made for almost nothing, they could not be sold so cheap when finished.

The facilities which the Jerome Manufacturing Company had over every other concern of the kind in the country, and their customers in this and foreign countries, are worth to the present company more than one hundred thousand dollars. Their method of making dials, tablets and brass doors was a saving of more than ten thousand dollars per year over any other company doing the same amount of business; and I know that the present company would not give up the customers of the Jerome Manufacturing Company for ten thousand dollars per year: they could not afford to do it. The workmen who came with me from Bristol, were an uncommonly energetic and ingenious set of men. Many years they had large and profitable jobs in the different branches, which encouraged them to invent and get up improvements for doing the work fast, and in a great many things they far surpass the workmen in similar establishments—all of which have resulted to the benefit of the present manufacturing company of New Haven.

In the year 1850, I was induced by a proposition from the Benedict & Burnham Co., of Waterbury, to enter into a joint-stock company at my place in New Haven, under the name of the Jerome Manufacturing Co. They were to put in thirty-five thousand dollars, and I was to furnish the same amount of capital. We did so, and went on very prosperously for a year or two, making a great many clocks, and selling about one hundred and fifty thousand dollars worth per year in England, at a profit of twenty thousand dollars. They were very thorough in looking into the affairs of the company, which was all right of course, but did not suit all of the interested parties. My son was Secretary and financial manager of the company. He seemed to have a desire to keep things to himself a little too much, which also did not suit many of the interested parties. My son told me he thought we had better buy the company out, and said that we could do so without difficulty, and he thought it would be a great advantage to us. Some were willing to sell, and others were not. Mr. Burnham made an offer what he would sell for, which the secretary accepted, others of the stock-holders made similar propositions and the bargain closed, we paying them the capital they had advanced and twenty-one per cent. profits, and buying, in the mean time, seventy-five thousand dollars worth of brass—the profits on which were not less than twenty thousand dollars, which they had the cash for in the course of the year. About this time a man by the name of Lyman Squires bought stock in the company, and took a great interest in the business. A wealthy brother of his bought, I think, ten thousand dollars worth of stock. The stock was increased in this way to two hundred thousand dollars. The financial affairs were managed by the Secretary, Mr. Squires, and a man by the name of Bissell. They made a great many additions to the factory which I thought quite unnecessary, enlarging the buildings, putting in a new engine and a great deal of costly machinery. They laughed at me because I found fault with these things and called me an old fogy. I was not pleased with the management at all times, and although I had retired from active busines, I felt a deep interest in the affairs of the company, and owned a large amount of the stock. The Secretary thought I was always looking on the dark side and prophesying evil, because I frequently remonstrated with him on the many extravagancies which were constantly being added to the establishment. I frequently told him that if the company should fail, I should have to bear the whole blame, because my name was known all over the world. He always told me in the strongest terms that I need give myself no uneasiness about that, as the company was worth a great deal of money. Things went on in this way till the year 1855, and while I was absent from the State, P. T. Barnum was admitted as a member of our company. Within six months from that time, the Jerome Manufacturing Company failed, the causes of which, and the results, I have clearly and truthfully narrated in another part of this book. The causes were not fully understood by me at that time. I have found them out since, and deem it an act of justice to myself to make them public. I was hopelessly ruined by this failure. The company had used my name as endorser to a large amount, many times larger than I had any idea of.

CHAPTER IX.

THE NEW HAVEN CLOCK COMPANY, AND OTHER CLOCK MANUFACTURERS IN CONNECTICUT.

I will here give a brief account of the firms carrying on this important business in Connecticut. The New Haven Clock Company, which succeeded the Jerome Manufacturing Company, are now making more clocks than any three other makers in the state. As I speak of the different manufactories, I will give the outlines and standing of the men connected with them. As their goods go all over the world, it is natural and pleasant for men who are dealing in their goods to know what kind of men they are at home, and what the community think of them. The New Haven company is a joint-stock company. The head man in this concern, is the Hon. James English, who is second to no business man in the State—high minded, clear sighted, and very popular with all who deal with him. He was, when a boy, remarkable for industry, prudence and good behavior. He was an apprentice at the house-joiner trade, but soon got into other business which gave him a greater chance to develope and become more useful to himself and the community. He began in life without a dollar, but is now said to be worth three hundred thousand dollars His age at this time is about forty-eight. He is a Democrat in politics; has been elected to many important offices, and has been the first select man of New Haven for many years; he has been elected State Senator for three years in succession, and all of these offices he has filled with ability. In the spring of 1860, he was nominated as candidate for Lieutenant Governor on a ticket with Col. Thomas H. Seymour of Hartford, for Governor, which made the most popular Democratic ticket that has ever been run in the State. Had it not been for the great anti-slavery feeling there was at this canvass, Mr. English would have been triumphantly elected. Many of the opposing party would been glad to have seen him elected, and would have voted for him, had it not been for the influence they thought it would have on the Presidential election. We heard many Republicans say this in New Haven, and many did vote that ticket.

H. M. Welch, who has for a long time been connected with Mr. English in business, is largely interested in this clock company. He gives most of his attention to other kinds of manufacturing, in which Messrs. English and Welch, are very extensively engaged. Mr. Welch is one of the most intelligent, upright, and kind hearted business men in the whole State, and is admired as such by all who know him. He is also a Democrat in politics, very popular in his party, and is well qualified for any offices. He would make a good candidate for Governor or member of Congress. He is about forty-six years old, worth perhaps, two hundred thousand dollars; he has held many important offices, has been a Representative to the State Legislature for many years, and State Senator a number of times. He has recently been elected Mayor of the city, and has filled all of these offices with much talent.

John Woodruff, a member of Congress, elected for the second time from this district, is the next largest owner in this great brass clock business. He commenced to work at clocks with me when a boy only fifteen years old. He was a very uncommon boy, and is now an uncommon man, very popular among his fellow workmen, popular with Democrats, popular with Republicans, popular every where, and can be elected to Congress when there is five hundred majority against his party in his district.

Hiram Camp who is the next largest stockholder in this clock company, is forty-nine years old. He commenced making clocks with me at the age of seventeen, and is now President of the company. He is a Republican in politics, and has been chosen Representative from New Haven to the Legislature of the State. At this time he is Chief Engineer of the Fire Department, is very popular with his workmen, and highly respected by the whole community in which he lives. Many others who hold prominent positions in this great business in New Haven, first came here with me when I moved from Bristol. I should mention Philip Pond, an excellent man who left the business two or three years since, on account of his health, but who is now connected in the wholesale grocery business of the firm of Pond, Greenwood & Lester, in this city. Also Charles L. Griswold, now a bit and augur maker in the town of Chester, who began to work for me twenty years ago, when a boy. He was once a poor boy, but now is a talented and superior man. He has been a member of the Legislature, and has held many offices of trust.

L. F. Root, now a leading man in New Haven, came to work with me when quite young, nearly twenty years ago. He also has held many offices of trust, and filled them with great ability. I could mention many others, but cannot in this brief work speak of them as their merits deserve. It gives me pleasure to know that the business of the Jerome Manufacturing Company has fallen into such good hands.

The Benedict and Burnham Company, now making clocks in the city of Waterbury, under the name of the Waterbury Clock Company, is composed of a large number of the first citizens of that place. In politics nearly all of them are Republicans. The oldest man of the company is Deacon Aaron Benedict, now about seventy-five years old—a real "old Puritan, Christian gentleman." He has been Representative and State Senator many times—Mr. Burnham of New York, another member of this company, is well known to almost every body as one of the richest men in whole country. My brother, Noble Jerome, who is an excellent mechanic and as good a brass clock maker as can be found, is now making the movements for this company, and Edward Church, a first rate man and an excellent workman, is making their cases. He worked with me seventeen years at case making, and can do a good job. I cannot pass without speaking about another man of this company, Arad W. Welton Esq. He was one of my soldier companions in Capt. John Buckingham's company, which went to fight the British in 1813, at

New London, and in 1814 at New Haven. He stood very near me in the ranks. I shall never forget what pluck and courage he showed one night when the news was brought into camp that the enemy were landing from their ships. Our whole regiment was mustered in fifteen minutes, and on the way to pitch battle with the British and defend our shores. This Mr. Welton, who is now an old man, as stout and large as Gen. Cass, and looking something like him, was then a young man nineteen years old, and without exception the funniest and drollest fellow that I ever saw. He kept us all laughing while we were going down to fight that awful battle, which, however, proved to be bloodless. This incident occurred at New London, and I have often thought of it in latter days. Mr. Welton is said to be a great business man, and the company with which he is connected is doing a good business.

The next clock company which I shall speak of, is that of Seth Thomas & Co., of Plymouth Hollow, Connecticut. As I have mentioned before, the senior Thomas is not living. The business is carried on by a company, the members of which are all Republicans in politics and respectable men. Fifty years ago this spring, Heman Clark built the factory which Seth Thomas, two or three years afterwards, bought, and in which he carried on business until his death, about two years since. It was never Mr. Thomas' practice to get up any thing new. He never would change his patterns or mode of manufacturing, until he was driven to it to keep his customers. At the time when I invented the one-day brass clock in 1838, he said much against it, that it was not half so good as a wood clock, and that he never would take up any thing again that Jerome had adopted; but he was compelled to, in a year or two, to keep his customers. He sent his foreman over to Bristol, where I was then carrying on business, to get patterns of movements and cases and take all the advantage he could of my experience, labors, and improvements which I had been studying upon so long. I allowed my foreman to spend more than two days with his, giving him all the knowledge and insight he could of the business, knowing what his object was. A friend asked me why I was doing this, and said that if I should send my man to Thomas' factory he would be kicked out immediately. I told him I knew that perfectly well, but that if Mr. Thomas set out to get into the business, he certainly would find out, and that the course I was taking was wisest and more friendly. I have thought since how quickly such kind treatment as I showed towards his man can be forgotten; yes; this company have all forgotten the service that I rendered them twenty years ago, and as I have said before, would probably have been making the old wood clock to this day, had it not been for other parties. There always has been a great deal of jealousy among the Yankee clock-makers, and they all seemed to hate the one who took the lead. The next establishment of which I shall speak, is that of William L. Gilbert, of Winsted, Connecticut. He is said to be miserly in feeling, and is quite rich; not very enterprising, but has made a great deal of money by availing himself of the improvements of others.

The next one in the business to whom I shall allude is E. N. Welch, of Bristol, Connecticut. He is about fifty years of age, and has been in many kinds of business. He was deeply interested in the failure of J. C. Brown a few years ago, and succeeded him in the clock business. He is a leading man in the Baptist church, and has a great tact for making money; but he says that all he wants of money is to do good with it. He is a Democrat in politics, and never wants an office from his party.

These five companies which I have named, make nearly all of the clocks manufactured in

Connecticut; though movements are made by three other companies. Beach and Hubbell of Bristol, are largely engaged in manufacturing the movements of brass marine clocks. Also two brothers by the name of Manross, in Bristol, are engaged in the same business. Noah Pomeroy of Bristol, is also engaged in making pendulum movements for other parties. I should, however, mention Ireneus Atkins, of Bristol, who is making a first-rate thirty-day brass clock, and I am told there is no better one for time in the country. The movement for this kind of clock was invented by Joseph Ives, who has spent most of his time for the last twenty-five years in improving on springs and escapements for clocks, and who has done a great deal for the advancement of this business. Mr. Atkins, who is making this thirty-day time-piece, is an excellent man to deal with. The five large companies which I have named, manufacture about a half a million clocks per annum; the New Haven company about two hundred thousand; and the others about three hundred thousand between them.

CHAPTER X.

BARNUM'S CONNECTION WITH THE JEROME CLOCK CO.—CAUSES AND RESULTS OF ITS FAILURE.

The connection of Barnum with the Jerome Manufacturing Company of New Haven, and the failure of the Company have been the subject of much speculation to the whole world, and has never been clearly understood. Barnum claimed that he was cheated and swindled by this company, robbed of his property and name, and reduced to poverty. But before giving any statements, I call attention to the following article taken from the New York Daily *Tribune*, of March 24th, 1860:

THE GREAT SHOWMAN.—P. T. Barnum, "the great American showman," as he loves to hear himself called, who furnishes more amusement for a quarter of a dollar than any other man in America, is, we are happy to announce, himself again. He has disposed of the last of those villainous clock notes, re-established his credit upon a cash basis, and once more comes forward to cater for the public amusement at the American museum. To day, between the acts of the play, Mr. Barnum will appear upon his own stage, in his own costly character of the Yankee Clockmaker, for which he qualified himself, with the most reckless disregard of expense, and will "give a brief history of his adventures as a clockmaker, showing how the clock ran down, and how it was wound up; shadowing forth in the same the future of the museum." Of course, Barnum's benefit will be a bumper. Next week the Museum will be closed for renovation and repairs, and the week after it will reopen under the popular P. T. B., once more.

I will now give the true statement of facts and particulars of his connection with the Jerome Manufacturing Company—which, however, was not his first experience in clock-making. Some time before this, he was interested in a Company located in the town of Litchfield, Connecticut, and, I believe, owned about ten thousand dollars worth of stock. They made a very poor article which was called a marine clock, if I am rightly informed. That Company failed, and Barnum took the stock as security for endorsing and furnishing them with cash. I do not suppose the whole of the effects were worth transporting to Bridgeport, although estimated by him at a large amount. About this time Theodore Terry's clock factory, at Ansonia, was destroyed by fire. A large portion of the stock was saved, though in a damaged condition, much of which was worth nothing—the tools and machinery being but little better than so much old iron. Terry knowing that Barnum was largely interested in real estate in East Bridgeport, and anxious to have it improved, thought he could make a good arrangement with him for building a factory there for the manufacture of clocks, and did so. Terry had a large quantity of old clocks in a store in New York—many of them old-fashioned and unsaleable, and thousands of these were not worth fifty cents apiece. Terry and Barnum now proposed forming a joint-stock company, putting in their old rubbish as stock, and estimating it, most likely, at four times its value in cash. They built a factory in East Bridgeport, and made preparations for manufacturing. Terry knew ten times as much about the business as Barnum did, and knowing, also, that the old stock was comparatively worthless, held back while Barnum was urging him to push ahead with the manufacturing. Terry made a great bluster, saying that he was going to hire men and do a great business, while, unknown to Barnum, he was trying to sell the stock he held in the company. They finally cooked up a plan to sell their New York store and the Bridgeport factory and machinery, if they could, to the Jerome Manfacturing Company, taking stock in that company for pay, and—the Jerome Company stock being issued to the owners of the Terry & Barnum stock—thus merge the two companies into one. This transaction was made and closed without my knowledge, (I being at the time from the State,) though the "old man" has had to bear all the blame. As I afterwards found out, Barnum told my son, the Secretary of the Company, that Terry & Barnum owed about twenty thousand dollars: this was the amount Terry had drawn for on the New York store. They made a written agreement with the Jerome Manufacturing Company, to this effect;—that our Company should assume the liabilities of their old Company, which were stated at twenty thousand dollars, and Barnum was to endorse to any extent for the Jerome Company. It afterwards proved that the entire debts of Terry & Barnum amounted to about seventy-two thousand dollars, which the Jerome Company were obliged to assume. The great difference in the real and supposed amount of their indebtedness and the unsaleable property turned in as stock were enough to ruin any company. It is a positive fact that the stock of the Jerome Company was not worth half as much, three months after Barnum came into the concern as it was before that time. Some of the stock-holders did not like to have Terry own stock, and Barnum to satisfy them, bought him out, paying him twelve thousand dollars in cash—he in the end, making a grand thing out his Ansonia remains. It is well known that the Jerome Manufacturing Company failed in the fall of 1855, to the wonder and astonishment of myself and of every body else. The true causes of this great failure never have been made public. I myself did not know them at that time, but have found them out from time to time since, and I now propose to make them public, as it has been the general impression almost every where that Barnum and myself were associated in defrauding the community. *I wish to have it understood that I never saw P. T. Barnum*, while he was connected with the Company of which I was a member. have never seen him but once since, and that was in February after the failure. About this time law suits were being brought against him, and as some supposed, by his friends. He was called upon, or offered himself as a witness, and I believe testified that he was worth nothing. The natural effect of this testimony was to depreciate the paper which his name was on. At the time when I saw him, he told me that the Museum was his just as much as it ever was, and that he received the profits, which had never been less than twenty-five thousand and were sometimes thirty thousand dollars per annum; and yet, he was publicly stating that he was worth nothing! He also, as I supposed, held securities of the Jerome Manufacturing Company, to a large amount, (as I suppose about one hundred thousand dollars,) for I know that such papers had been in his hands. There were many persons who were interested in the revival of the business, who were in some way flattered into the belief that Barnum would re-purchase the whole clock establishment and put them back into the business again. Several men were sent by some one to examine the property and estimate its value, and those persons who were anxious for a restoration of the business were in some way led to believe that Barnum intended to re-commence the business of clock-making. For myself, I do not suppose that Barnum ever seriously contemplated any such thing; but the belief that he did, made some men quiet who might otherwise have been active and troublesome.

The manner in which this matter has been represented would reflect dishonesty upon the Secretary, which would be untrue. No one who knows him will, or can accuse him of dishonesty. I love truth, honesty and religion; I do not mean, however, the religion that Barnum believes in: (I believe that the wicked are punished in another world.) I ask the reader to look at my situation in my old age. I think as much of a good name, as to purity of character and honesty at heart, as any man living; and very often reading in the New York papers of speeches that Barnum has made, alluding to his being defrauded by the Jerome Manufacturing Company, I wish the world to know the whole facts in the case, and what my position was in the Company which bore my name. After many years—years of very active business life—I had retired from active duty in the Company, although I took a deep interest in every thing connected with it, and also a great pride, as it was a business that I had built up and had been many years in perfecting. The manufacturing had been systematized in the most perfect manner and every thing looked prosperous to me. I owned stock as others did, but did not know of its financial standing, and was always informed that it was all right, and that I should be perfectly safe in endorsing. I wish to have it understood that I did not sign my name to any of this paper, it being done by the Secretary himself, that therefore I could not know of the amounts that were raised in that way, that I did not find out till after the failure, and then the large amounts overwhelmed me with surprise.

It will be remembered that Barnum made two or three trips to Europe to provide in some way for the support of his "poor and destitute" family, which as he claimed, had been robbed and ruined by the Connecticut clock-makers. At one time he was stopped on a pier in New York, just as he was starting for Europe, by a suit brought against him. Thus the news went abroad that poor Barnum was hunted and troubled on every side with these clock notes. It was reported that he was quite sick in England and could not live, and, at another time, that being much depressed and discouraged on account of his many troubles, he had taken to drinking very hard, and in all probability would live but a short time; while at the same time, he was lecturing on temperance to the English people, and was in fact a total-abstinence man. These stories were extensively circulated; the value of his paper was depreciated in the market, and was, in several instances bought for a small sum.

Since writing the foregoing with regard to his coming into the Company, and, as he states, being ruined by it, I have ascertained to my own satisfaction, that our connection with him was the means of ruining the Company. A few days since I was talking with a man who has been more familiar than myself with the whole transaction, and he told me it was his opinion that if we had never seen Barnum we should still have been making clocks in that factory. It was a great mystery to me, and to every body else, how the Company could run down so rapidly during the last year. I think I have found out, and these are my reasons. Instead of having an amount of twenty thousand dollars to cancel of the Terry & Barnum debts and accounts (which the Secretary foolishly agreed to do,) it eventually proved to be about seventy thousand; (this I have found out since the failure.) This great loss the Secretary kept to himself, and it involved the Company so deeply that he became almost desperate; for knowing by this time that he had been greatly embarrassed, he was determined to raise money in any way that he could, honestly, and get out of the difficulty if possible. He had, as he thought, got to keep this an entire secret, because if known it would ruin the credit of the Company. When these extra drafts and notes of Terry & Barnum were added to the debts of the Company, he was obliged to resort to various expedients to raise money to pay them. This led him to the exchange of notes on a large scale, which proved to be a great loss, as many of the parties were irresponsible. There was a loss of thirty thousand dollars by one man, and I am sure that there must have been more than fifty thousand dollars lost in this way. He was also obliged to issue short drafts and notes and raise money on them at fearful rates. The Terry & Barnum stock which was taken in at par, was not worth twenty-five per cent. which had a tendency to reduce the value of the stock of our Company, though I have recently heard that the Secretary bought stock at par for the Jerome Company of some former owners in the Terry & Barnum Company, in Bridgeport, only a short time before the failure. To show the confidence the Secretary had in the standing of the Company, he recommended one of his own brothers, not more than one month before the Company failed, to buy five thousand dollars worth of the stock, which he did. It was owned by a Bridgeport man and he paid par value for it in good gold and silver watches at cash prices. All of these transactions were made without my knowledge, and I have found them out by piece-meal ever since. I do fully believe that if the Secretary had been worth half a million of dollars, he would have sacrificed every dollar, rather than have had the Company failed under his management as it did.

It has been publicly stated that Mr. Barnum endorsed largely on blank notes and drafts and that he was thus rendered responsible to a far greater extent than he was aware of; such, however, was not the case.

The troubles that have grown out of the failure of this great business, have left me poor and broken down in spirit, constitution and health. I was never designed by Providence to eat the bread of dependence, for it is like poison to me, and will surely kill me in a short time. I have now lost more than forty pounds of flesh, though my ambition has not yet died within me.

CHAPTER XI.

EFFECTS OF THE FAILURE ON MYSELF.—REMOVAL TO WATERBURY AND ANSONIA.—UNFORTUNATE BUSINESS CONNECTIONS, ETC.

After saying so much as I have about my misfortunes in life, I must say a few words about what has happened and what I have been through with during the last four years.

When the Jerome Manufacturing Company failed, every dollar that I had saved out of a long life of toil and labor was not enough to support my family for one year. It was hard indeed for a man sixty-three years old, and my heart sickened at the prospect ahead. Perhaps there never was a man that wanted more than I did to be in business and be somebody by the side of my neighbors. There never was a man more grieved than I was when I had to give up those splendid factories with the great facilities they had over all others in the world for the manufacture of clocks both good and cheap, all of which had been effected through my untiring efforts. No one but myself can know what my feelings were when I was compelled, through no fault of my own, to leave that splendid clustre of buildings with all its machinery, and its thousands of good customers all over this country and Europe, and in fact the whole world, which in itself was a fortune. And then to leave that beautiful mansion at the head of the New Haven bay, which I had almost worshipped. I say to leave all these things for others, with that spirit and pride that still remained within me, and at my time of life, was almost too much for flesh and blood to bear. What could have been the feelings of my family, and my large circle of friends and acquaintances, to see creditors and officers coming to our house every day with their pockets full of attachments and piles of them on the table every night. If any one can ever begin to know my feelings at this time, they must have passed through the same experience. Yet mortified and abused as I was, I had to put up with it. Thank God, I have never been the means of such trouble for others. I had to move to Waterbury in my old age, and there commence again to try to get a living. I moved in the fall of 1856, and as bad luck would have it, rented a house not two rods from a large church with a very large steeple attached to it, which had been built but a short time before. In one of the most terrific hurricanes and snow storms that I ever knew in my life, at four o'clock in the morning of January 19th, 1857, this large steeple fell on the top of our house which was a three story brick building. It broke through the roof and smashed in all the upper tier of rooms, the bricks and mortar falling to the lower floor. We were in the second story, and some of the bricks came into our room, breaking the glass and furniture, and the heaviest part of the whole lay directly on our house. It was the opinion of all who saw the ruins that we did not stand one chance in ten thousand of not being killed in a moment. I heard many a man say he would not take the chances that we had for all the money in the State. One man in the other part of the house was so frightened that he was crazy for a long time. Timbers in this steeple, ten inches square, broke in two directly over my bed and their weight was tremendous. I now began to think that my troubles were coming in a different form; but it seems I was not to die in that way. The business took a different shape in the spring, and I moved (another task of moving!) to Ansonia. Here I lived two years, but very unfortunately happened to get in with the worst men that could be found on the line of Rail-road between Winsted and Bridgeport. In another part of this book I have spoken of them; I do not now wish to think of them, for it makes me sick to see their names on paper. I had worked hard ever since I left New Haven—one year at Waterbury, and two at this place (Ansonia,)—but got not one dollar for the whole time. I was robbed of all the money which Mr. Stevens, (my son-in-law,) had paid me for the use of my trade-mark in England, for the years 1857-'58. This advantage was taken of me, because I could collect nothing in my own name.

I should consider my history incomplete, unless I went back for many years to speak of the treatment which I received from a certain man. I shall not mention his name, and my object in relating these circumstances is to illustrate a principle there is in man, and to caution the young men to be careful when they get to be older and are carrying on business, not to do too much for one individual. If you do, in nine cases out of ten, he will hate and injure you in the end. This has been my experience. Many years ago, I hired two men from a neighboring town to work for me. It was about the time that I invented the Bronze Looking-Glass Clock, which was, at that time, decidedly the best kind made. After a while these two men contrived a plan to get up a company, go into another town, and manufacture the same kind of clock. This company was formed about six months before I found it out, and much of their time was spent in making small tools and clock-parts to take with them. This was done when they were at work for me on wages. They induced as many of my men as they could to go with them, and took some of them into company. When they had finished some clocks, they went round to my customers and under-sold me to get the trade. This is the first chapter. When I invented the thirty-hour brass clock in 1838, one of these men had returned to Bristol again, and was out of business; but he had some money which he had made out of my former improvements. I had lost a great deal of money in the great panic of 1837. After I had started a little in making this new clock, he proposed to put in some money and become interested with me, and as I was in want of funds to carry on the business, I told him that if he would put in three thousand dollars, he should have a share of the profits. I went on with him one year, but got sick of it and bought him out. I had to pay six thousand dollars to get rid of him. He took this money, went to a neighboring town, bought an old wood clock factory, fitted it up for making the same clock that I had just got well introduced, and induced several of my workmen to go with him, some of whom he took in company with him. As soon as I had the clock business well a going in England, he sent over two men to sell the same patterns. He has kept this up ever since, and has made a great deal of money.

After the failure of the Jerome Manufacturing Company, as I have already stated, I went to Waterbury to assist the Benedict & Burnham Company. After I had been there six or eight months, and had got the case-making well started, (my brother, Noble Jerome, had got the movements in the works the year before,) this same man I have been speaking about, came to me and made me a first-rate offer to go with him into a town a short distance from Waterbury, and make clocks there. I accepted his offer, but should not have done so, had it not been for the depressed condition to which I had been brought by previous events. I accordingly moved to the town where he had hired a factory. He was carrying on the business at the same time in his old factory, and came to this new place about twice a week. My work was in the third story, and it was very hard for an old man to go up and down a dozen times a day. About this time I obtained a patent on a new clock case, and as I was to be interested in the business, I let the Company make several thousand of them. We could make forty cents more on each clock than we could on an O-G. clock. As I was favorably known throughout the world as a clock-maker, this Company wanted to use my label as the clocks would sell better in some parts of the country than with his label. They were put upon many thousands. Soon after we commenced, I told him I would make out a writing of our bargain because life was uncertain. He said that was all right, and that he would attend to it soon. As he always seemed to be in a hurry when he came, I wrote one and sent it to him, so that he might look it over at his leisure and be ready to sign it when he came down again. The next time I saw him, I asked him if the writing was not as we agreed; he said he supposed it was, but that he had no time to look it over and sign it then, but would do so when he had time. I paid into the business about one thousand nine hundred dollars in small sums, as it was wanted from time to time, and worked at this man for eight months to get a writing from him, but he always had an excuse. He had agreed to give the case-maker a share of the profits if he would make the cases at a certain price, but put him off in the same way. We both became satisfied that he did not mean to do as he had agreed, and I therefore left him. The money which I had paid in was what I had received for the use of my name in England. I had the privilege of paying it in as it was wanted, working eight months, keeping the accounts which I did evenings, and giving this man a home at my house whenever he was in town. All of this which I had done, he refused to give me one dollar for, and it was with great difficulty that I got my money back. I had to put it into another man's hands, as his property, to recover it. This man, probably, had two objects in view when he went to Waterbury to flatter me away. He did not want me to be there with my name on the movements and cases, and therefore he made me a first-rate offer. I had been broken up in all my business, and felt very anxious to be doing something again. I was a little afraid when he made the offer, but knew that he had made a great deal of money out of my improvements and was very wealthy, and I did think he would be true to me, knowing as he did my circumstances. Look at this miser, with not a child in the world, and no one on earth that he cares one straw about, and yet so grasping! Oh! what will the poor creature do in eternity!

CHAPTER XII.

MORE MISPLACED CONFIDENCE.—ANOTHER UNFORTUNATE PARTNERSHIP.

Before closing the history of the many trials and troubles which I have experienced during my life, I will here say that I have never found, in all my dealings with men for more than forty years, such an untruthful and dishonest a man as * * * of a certain town in Connecticut. In 1858, he induced me to come into his factory to carry on a little business. My situation was such, in consequence of the failure of the Jerome Manufacturing Company, that I could do nothing in my own name, as he knew. I had a little money that had been paid me for the use of my trademark in England, and I felt very anxious, as old as I was, to make a little money so that I could pay some small debts which my family had made a short time before the company failed. I had also two children who looked to me for some help. This man said to me, "you may have the use of my factory for 'so much,' and you may carry on the business for one year in my name for so 'much.' This was agreed to by both parties. In a few days he came to me and said that he had been talking with his nephew about having the business carried on in his name " & Co. ;" * * * being the "Company" and he was to keep his nephew harmless, as he had nothing for the use of his name. The nephew came into the factory a short time after, and I asked him if he had agreed to what * * * had stated to me; he said that he had, and that I could go on with the business in the name of himself & Co.; he was quite sure that his uncle would keep him harmless. I went on with the business in this name from May to December, both of those men knowing all the while just as much about the business as I did, and they never said but that it was all right as we had agreed. I paid in my money from time to time as it was wanted. Late in the fall, I paid in at one time, one thousand nine hundred dollars, through a firm who owed me that amount, and who gave their notes to * * * on short time, which notes were paid. A short time after this, knowing that I had no more money to put into the business, he undoubtedly thought it time to do what he had intended to do at a suitable time from the beginning. One day when I was unwell and confined to the house, a man who had a claim against the company, called on * * * to make a settlement. Before this time he had made two payments on this same account, but he now told this man that there never had been such a company, and that he would never pay it—while at the same time, he had the same property which the man offered to take back but which he had refused to give up, and said that I had no right to use the name of——& Co. This was after he had been using the name for me in drafts and notes, and all other business transactions, for more than eight months. He said that he would have me arrested for fraud and put in the State Prison. This treatment was rather hard towards a man who had never before been accused of dishonesty, and who had done business on a large scale with thousands of men for more than forty years. He at one time requested me to borrow a note for him from one of my friends, which I did, and which he paid promptly when due. He did this, as I now suppose, because the business was not in as good shape for him as it might be in another three months; so he wished me to get the favor renewed, which I did. When it became due, he denied that it was a borrowed note, declared that I was owing him, and had handed this note to him as one that was good and would be paid. One of his best friends has since told me that there was more honor among horse-thieves than this man had shown towards me. I put into the business between four and five thousand dollars, worked hard almost a year, and have received about five hundred dollars. * * * is trying to scare me by threatening to sue me for perjury; so that if he could make me fool enough to pay the debts of ———— & Co., he would have just so much more to put into his own pocket. When he can get a grand jury to find a true bill against me for fraud or perjury, I will promise to go to Wethersfield and stay there the remainder of my life, without any further trial. After all that I have said, I think of him just as all his neighbors do; for they have told me that it was the common talk among them, when I first went into his factory, that he would in some way cheat me out of every dollar that I put into his hands. It would take just about as much evidence to prove that young crows would be black when their feathers are grown, as it would to satisfy the community that these statements are true, especially where he is known. For knavery, untruthfulness, and wickedness, I have never seen anything, in all my business experience of forty years, that will compare with this. He would not have taken such a course with me once, but he took advantage of my age and misfortunes to commit these frauds, thinking that I could not defend myself, and that he could defraud and crush me.

I had paid every dollar of my money into this business which I had at that time, and had nothing to live on through the winter. But John Woodruff in his kindness, raised money enough for me to live on through the winter, and the following spring I moved to New Haven.

CHAPTER XIII.

THE WOOSTER PLACE CHURCH.—GROWTH OF THE DIFFERENT DENOMINATIONS IN NEW HAVEN.

In order to have my history complete I must give my reason for building the Wooster Place Church, as my motives have been misconstrued by many persons, I will make a short statement of what I know to be true. It is well known that with the exception of one, all the Congregational churches in New Haven, were located west of the centre of the city. The majority of the inhabitants lived in the eastern section. Meeting after meeting was called by the different churches to consider the importance of building a church in the eastern part. It was strongly advocated by the ministers and many others, that this part of the city was rapidly filling up, a great deal of manufacturing was carried on there, and the strangers who were constantly coming in would fall into other denominations. I heard their speeches advocating this course with great pleasure, as I lived in the eastern part of the city, had a long distance to go to attend church, and nearly all the workmen in my employ lived in the same section. The church which I have mentioned as the only one located east of the centre, was in a very prosperous condition. By the talent, popularity and piety of its minister, as his church and congregation believed, he had filled the church to overflowing. There were no slips to be bought in that church. We heard this minister say that he could spare thirty families from his congregation to build up a new church. In view of all the facts, I started a subscription paper, in as good faith as I ever did anything in my life, for the raising of funds to build an edifice. The subscription was headed by myself with five thousand dollars and many large sums were added to it. A number of wealthy men lived near the contemplated place of building the new church, who belonged to other churches. It was supposed, by what their ministers had said in public and in private, that they would use their influence in advancing this good work, and to have some of their members join in it; but for some reason they changed their minds. I heard that the minister of the church located in the eastern section (which I mentioned before,) had got up a subscription paper to raise ten or twelve thousand dollars to beautify the front of his church, raise a higher steeple, and make some other alterations that he thought important. I was told that he called on the men who lived in the locality where we proposed erecting the new church, with his subscription, and that they subscribed to carry out his plans. Some of those who had subscribed to build the new church, after he had made these calls, wrote me that they wished their names crossed off from my paper— Others came and told me the same thing, and wished their names erased. I began at this time to understand that there were influences working against our enterprise and that this way of building a church must be given up. I however, went forward myself, as is very well known, and built a church second to none in New England. I should have built one that would not have cost one half of the money, had I acted on my own judgement, but I was influenced by a few others differently. I paid more than twenty thousand dollars out of my own pocket into this church.

Public opinion in the community was, that if the several ministers had given their influence in favor of this matter, a church would have been built by subscription. They could very easily have influenced their friends in that part of the city to unite in this enterprise without detriment to their own congregation. Had this course been taken, it is evident that by this time it would have been a large and prosperous church.

A correspondent of the Independent in writing upon the growth of Congregationalism, in New Haven, had a great deal to say about the Wooster Place church—calling the man that built it, "a sagacious mechanic, who built it on speculation etc." Yet ; added "if they had called a young man for its Pastor from New England, it might have succeeded after all."

It is well known that the Congregational denomination has made but very small advancement compared with others for the last twenty years. It is supposed that the inhabitants of New Haven have doubled in number during that time; but only one small Mission church has been added to the Congregational churches. Four Episcopal churches have been built, and filled with worshipers, many of whom formerly belonged to Congregational families. The Methodists have built two large churches, and more than trebled in number. The Baptists have more than doubled, and now own and occupy the Wooster Place church. And to have kept pace with the others, the Congregational denomination should now have as many as three more large churches.

CHAPTER XIV

NEW HAVEN AS A BUSINESS PLACE.—GROWTH—EXTENSIVE MANUFACTORIES, ETC.

For many years I have extensively advertised throughout every part of the civilized world, and in the most conspicuous places, such a city as New Haven Connecticut, U. S. A., and its name is hourly brought to notice wherever American clocks are used, and I know of no more conspicuous or prominent place than the dial of a clock for this purpose. More of these clocks have been manufactured in this city for the past sixteen years than any other one place in this country, and the company now manufacturing, turn out seven hundred daily.

I now propose to give a brief description of New Haven and its inhabitants in the words of a business man who loves the town. New Haven, is to-day a city of more than forty thousand inhabitants, remarkable as the New Englanders generally are for their ingenuity, industry, shrewd practical good sense, and their large aggregate wealth; and with forty thousand such people it is not strange that New Haven is now growing like a city in the west. It was settled in 1638, and incorporated as a city in 1784. Its population in 1830, was less than eleven thousand, and in 1840, but little more than fourteen thousand, its increase from 1840 to 1850, was about eight thousand, and from 1850 to 1860, the population has nearly doubled. The assessed value of property in 1830, amounted to about two and a half millions. The amount at the present time is estimated at over twenty seven millions. New Haven is situated at the head of a fine bay, four miles from Long Island Sound, and seventy-six miles from New York, on the direct line of Rail-road, and great thoroughfare between that city and Boston, and can be reached in three hours by Railroad and about five by water from New York. New Haven has long been known as the city of Elms, and it far surpasses any other city in America in the number and beauty of these noble elm trees which shade and adorn its streets and public squares. It is a place of large manufacturing interests, the persevering genius and enterprise of its people having made New Haven in a variety of ways, prominent in industrial pursuits. Mr. Whitney, the inventor of the Cotton Gin, Mr. Goodyear of india rubber notoriety, and many other great and good men who by their ingenuity and perseverance have added millions to the wealth of mankind, were citizens of New Haven. Nearly every kind of manufactured article known in the market, can here be found and bought direct from the manufactory—such as carriages and all kind of carriage goods, firearms, shirts, locks, furniture, clothing, shoes, hardware, iron castings, daguerrotype-cases, machinery, plated goods, &c., &c.

The manufacture of carriages is here carried on, on a grand scale, and its yearly productions are probably larger than of any other city in the Union. There are more than sixty establishments in full operation at the present time, many of them of great extent and completeness, and turn out work justly celebrated for its beauty and substantial value wherever they are known. I live in the immediate vicinity of the largest carriage manufactury in the world, which turns out a finished carriage every hour; much of the work being done by machinery and systematized in much the same manner as the clock-making. American carriages are fast following American clocks to foreign countries, to the West Indies, Australia and the Sandwich Islands, Mexico and South America, and I believe the day is not far distant when they will be exported to Europe in large quantities, and the present prospect seems far more favorable for them than it did for me when I introduced my first cargo of clocks into England.

When I first saw this city in 1812, its population was less than five thousand, and it looked to me like a country town. I wandered about the streets early one morning with a bundle of clothes and some bread and cheese in my hands little dreaming that I should live to see so great a change, or that it ever would be my home. I remember seeing the loads of wood and chips for family use lying in front of the houses, and acres of land then in cornfields and valued at a small sum, are now covered with fine buildings and stores and factories in about the heart of the city.

When I moved my case making business to New Haven, the project was ridiculed by other clock-makers, of going to a city to manufacture by steam power, and yet it seems to have been the commencement of manufacturers in the country, coming to New Haven to carry on their business. Numbers came to me to get my opinion and learn the advantages it had over manufacturing in the country, which I always informed them in a heavy business was very great, the item of transportation alone overbalancing the difference between water and steam power. The facilities for procuring stock and of shipping, being also an important item. Not one of the good citizens will deny that this great business of clock-making which I first brought to New Haven has been of immense advantage and of great importance to the city. Through its agency millions of money has been brought here, adding materially to the general prosperity and wealth, besides bringing it into notice wherever its productions are sent. I have been told that there is nothing in the eastern world that attracts the attention of the inhabitants like a Yankee clock. It has this moment come into my mind of several years ago giving a dozen brass clocks to a missionary at Jerusalem; they were shipped from London to Alexandria in Egypt, from there to Joppa, and thence about forty miles on the backs of Camels to Jerusalem, where they arrived safe to the great joy of the missionary and others interested, and attracted a great deal of attention and admiration. I also sent my clocks to China, and two men to introduce them more than twenty years ago.

I will here say what I truly believe as to the future of this business; there is no place on the earth where it can be started and compete with

New Haven, there are no other factories where they can possibly be made so cheap. I have heard men ask the question, "why can't clocks be made in Europe on such a scale, where labor is so cheap?" If a company could in any part of the old world get their labor ten years for nothing, I do not believe they could compete with the Yankees in this business. They can be made in New Haven and sent into any part of the world for more than a hundred years to come for less than one half of what they could be made for in any part of the old world. I was many years in systematizing this business, and these things I know to be facts, though it might appear as strong language. No man has ever lived that has given so much time and attention to this subject as myself. For more than fifty years, by day and by night, clocks have been uppermost in my mind. The ticking of a clock is music to me, and although many of my experiences as a business man have been trying and bitter, I have the satisfaction of knowing that I have lived the life of an honest man, and have been of some use to my fellow men.

APPENDIX.

GENERAL DIRECTIONS FOR KEEPING CLOCKS IN ORDER.

Pendulum clocks are the oldest style, and are more generally introduced than any other kind. I will give a few simple suggestions essential for keeping this clock in good order as a time-keeper. In the first place, a clock must be plumb (that is level;) and what I mean by plumb, is not treing up the case to a level, but it is to put the case in a position so that the beats or sounds of the wheel-teeth striking the verge are equal. It is not necessary to go by the sound, if the face is taken off so that you can see the verge. You can then notice and see whether the verge holds on to the teeth at each end the same length of time; or (in other words) whether the vibrations are equal as they should be. Clocks are often condemned because they stop, or because they do not keep good time, while these points and others are not in beat, the vibrations are not regular; hence it will not divide the time equally, and it is called a poor time-keeper, when the difficulty may be that it is not properly set up. A clock which will run when it is much out of beat, is a very good one, and it must run very easily, because it has a great disadvantage to overcome, viz: a greater distance from a perpendicular line one way than the other in order that the verge may escape the teeth. A clock may be set up in perfect beat, but the shelf is liable to settle or warp, and get out of beat so gradually, that it might not be remarked by one not suspecting it, unless special notice was taken of it. This matter should be looked to when the clock stops.

I have explained the mode of setting up a clock with reference to putting it in beat, etc. Another essential point to be attended to is that the rod should hang in the centre or very near the centre of the loop in the crutch wire which is connected with the verge, and for this reason, if it rubs the front or back end of the loop, the friction will cause it to stop. To prevent this, set the clock case so that it will lean back a little or forward, as it requires. It sometimes happens that the dial (if it is made of zinc) gets bent in, and the loop of the crutch wire rubs as it passes back and forth. This should be attended to. It should be noticed also, whether the crutch wire gets misplaced so that it rubs any kind of a dial; the least impediment here will stop a clock. The centre of the dial should next be noticed. It sometimes happens that the warping moves it from its place, so that the sockets of the pointers rub, and many times it is the cause of the clock's stopping; this can be remedied by pareing out the centre on the side required.

Soft verges are no uncommon cause of clocks stopping, and those who travel to repair clocks generally overlook this trouble. A clock with a soft verge will run but a short time, because the teeth will dent into the face of the verge and cause a roughness that will certainly stop it. The way to ascertain this, is to try a file on the end of the verge; if you can file it it is soft; they are intended to be so hard that a file will not cut them. They can be hardened without taking off the brass ears or crutch wires, if you are careful in heating them; but the roughness on the faces caused by the teeth must be taken out in finishing. They must be polished nicely, and the polish lines should run parallel with the verge: this may not seem to some necessary, but if the polished lines run crosswise you can hear it rub distinctly and it would cause it to stop.

It is very common to hear a clock make a creaking noise, and this leads inexperienced persons to think it has become dry inside. This is not so, and you will always find it to be caused by the loop of the crutch wire where it touches the rod; apply a little oil and it will cure it.

Some think that a clock must be cleaned and oiled often, but if the foregoing directions are carefully pursued it is not necessary. I could show the reader several thirty-four hour brass clocks of my first and second years' manufacture (about twenty-two years since) which have been taken apart and cleaned but once—perhaps some of them twice. I have been told that they run as well as they did the first year. Now these are the directions which I should lay down for you to save your money, and your clocks from untimely wearing out. If you see any signs of their stopping—such as a faint beat, or if on a very cold night they stop, take the dial off, and the verge from the pin, wipe the pin that the verge hangs on, the hole in the ears of the verge, and the pieces that act on the wheel; also the loop of the verge wire where it connects with the rod, and the rod itself where the loop acts. Previous to taking off the verge, oil all the pivots in front; let the clock be wound up about half way, then take off the verge, and let it run down as rapidly as it will, in order to work out the gummy oil: then wipe off the black oil that has worked out and it is not necessary to add any more to the pivots. Then oil the parts as above described connected with the verge and be very sparing of the oil, for too little is better than too much. I never use any but watch oil. You may think that the other oils are good because you have tried them; but I venture to say that all the good they effected was temporary and after a short time the clock was more gummed up than it was before. Watch oil is made from the porpoise' jaw, and I have not seen anything to equal it. You may say why not oil the back pivots? They do not need it as often as the front ones, because they are not so much exposed, and hence, they do not catch the dust which passes through the sash and through the key holes that causes the pivots to be gummy and gritty. The front pivot holes wear largest first. A few pennys' worth of oil will last many years.

It is necessary to occasionally oil the pulleys on the top of the case which the cord passes over. If this is not done the hole becomes irregular, and a part of the power is lost to the clock. Common oil will answer for them. With regard to balance-wheel clocks, it is more difficult to explain the mode of repairing, to the inexperienced. With reference to oiling, use none but watch oil.

www.ingramcontent.com/pod-product-compliance
Lightning Source LLC
Chambersburg PA
CBHW030117170426
43198CB00009B/643